D0951920

Grateful acknowledgment is made for permission to reprint the following: "Ninon de Lenclos, On Her Last Birthday," *copyright 1931, renewed © 1959 by Dorothy Parker, from* The Portable Dorothy Parker *by Dorothy Parker. Introduction by Brendan Gill. Used by permission of Viking Penguin, a division of Penguin Books USA Inc.*
Lines from "The Shropshire Lad" by A.E. Housman. Used by permission of Branden Publishing Company.
Lines from "Poem in October" by Dylan Thomas. Poems of Dylan Thomas. *Copyright 1945 by the Trustees of the Copyrights of Dylan Thomas. Reprinted by permission of New Directions Publishers Corporation.*

Library of Congress Cataloging in Publication Data

Thompson, Sylvia Vaughn.
    The birthday cake book / by Sylvia Thompson; illustrated by Brooke Scudder.
        p.   cm.
    ISBN 0-8118-0227-2
    1. Cake.   I. Title.
    TX771.T49 1993   92-15076
    641.8'653-dc20   CIP

Printed in Hong Kong.

Distributed in Canada by Raincoast Books, 112 East Third Ave., Vancouver, B.C. V5T 1C8

10 9 8 7 6 5 4 3 2 1

Chronicle Books
275 Fifth Street
San Francisco, CA 94103

The Birthday Cake Book

By Sylvia Thompson

Illustrations By Brooke Scudder

CHRONICLE BOOKS

SAN FRANCISCO

For
Jacob
James
Dylan
Samuel
Weston
Deborah
Austin
Jasen
and the darlings to come
with love!

Acknowledgments

I wish to thank Dèan Mastromatteo for her skill, patience, and cheerfulness in testing these cakes and frostings for me on the flats. My thanks as well to Hildegard Manley (who has long since forgiven me for decorating her birthday cake with what I thought were the harmless blossoms of oleander), Lynnda Hart, and my mother, Jane Levy, generous friends and gifted cooks who also baked for me.

I couldn't be happier that Caroline Herter and Bill LeBlond entrusted this subject to me. And gave the manuscript an extraordinary copy editor, Carolyn Krebs. And chose the felicitous work of artist Brooke Scudder and designer Marianne Mitten.

Bantam Books graciously granted permission for me to do this book in the midst of my writing a magnum opus on the kitchen garden for them, and I am much obliged.

Susan Lescher knows I am grateful to her and why.

Every girl should have a husband like mine.

Now if only I could lose the twelve pounds....

The ancient Persians,
great pastry chefs,
were the first to bake special cakes for celebrations.
And Herodotus tells us that of all the days of the year,
the one the Persians most celebrated
was their birthday.

Contents

How to Bake a Perfect Birthday Cake

Why a Birthday Cake from Scratch?

Once I thought that homemade cakes—despite the leavening of all that love—were necessarily, well, heavier than those from box and baker. Tools of the trade, after all, are an arsenal of lighteners-brighteners-smoother-out-ers-everything-enhancers. A hundred cakes later, I know better. You hold in your hands recipes for cakes that will take your breath away with their lightness. And those that aren't meant to be airy-fairy will dazzle with their flavor. Beyond freshness, purity, and incomparable ingredients, there's heart in these cakes—the age-old ritual of creating something with your own hands on your own hearth. That adds immeasurably to the cake's luster (not to mention your own good karma).

Here are birthday cakes money can't buy. Some are Big Deals. Some are extra easy. Most are splurge cakes, on the theory that birthdays are infrequent and should be gala. All are fun to make and all are perfect Tens. For accompaniment, there's a master recipe for light European water ices made without a machine. You can't buy them, either. Unless the cake is such that any accompaniment would be superfluous, or unless ice cream is traditional, I've suggested the water ice I think best suits each cake.

Me? Make a Perfect Cake? How do I do that?

Directions in the recipes may seem detailed, but in the details lie success. Take the time. The lightest possible butter cake is made by the creaming method, the one our grandmothers and their grandmothers used. It takes about twenty minutes longer to make a classic batter than a dump-and-mix cake. Quick-mix cake is fine for a school outing, but for a splendid once a year occasion, I'm sure you'll cheerfully give the twenty extra minutes.

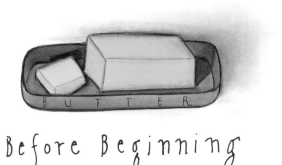

Before Beginning

Here's what you can do to ensure success.

WORK PEACEABLY AND NONSTOP. Air is the critical ingredient in cakes. Because the air you beat into batter starts escaping the instant you stop beating, time is of the essence. Take the phone off the hook and lock the kitchen door. Read through the recipe so there'll be no surprises. Once you've begun, even should an angel appear at the window, don't stop until your cake is in the oven.

USE THE VERY BEST INGREDIENTS. Soft-wheat cake flour bakes the tenderest cake, although closely knit cakes (gingercake, carrot cake) profit from the added gluten in all-purpose flour. Sift flour to lighten it before measuring (if your air is humid, sift two or three times)....The freshest and sweetest fat for cakes is unsalted butter....Many feel European dark chocolate has finer flavor (I'm not one of them)....And note there are two forms of cocoa in these recipes. Old-fashioned unsweetened Hershey's cocoa is nonalkalized, Dutch process or European style is alkalized. They are not interchangeable.... Renew ground spices and baking powder every six months, flour and cream of tartar annually. Store in tightly sealed jars in a cool dark dry place.

HAVE ALL INGREDIENTS AT OPTIMUM TEMPERATURE. Generally, all ingredients should be around 70°F....Soften butter to the consistency of mayonnaise in the microwave at half-power (in 5- to 10-second increments) or in a warmish place an hour or two—butter's temperature and texture are critical for creaming to maximum airiness....When warm, yolks and whites beat to maximum volume. Cover eggs in their shells in a bowl with hot tap water, then leave them until needed.

WORK WITH UTENSILS THAT ARE PLEASING so you'll enjoy yourself. Mixing bowls should be deep and beautiful....If you plan to make cakes often, buy a classic drum sifter. It has just one screen—three-screen sifters are the standard—but since the flour is tossed high in the air, I'm satisfied it has been amply lightened, and only a drum sifter makes sifting fun....My invaluable large flexible rubber spatula measures 4 1/2 by 2 3/4 inches.... Next time you see chopsticks, bring some home—nothing is more aesthetic for leveling measuring cups, stirring chocolate, making a banner of greeting.... An electric mixer is indispensable in beating air into batter. All the recipes in this book were created with a three-speed portable mixer six years old. I use a portable mixer because it moves easily from counter to stove, I have control over it, and it does the job.

MEASURE WITH CARE. For dry ingredients, use cups that come nested in 1/4-cup, 1/3-cup, 1/2-cup, and 1-cup measures. Measure by setting the appropriate cup over waxed paper and using a big spoon to lightly fill the cup, then sweep the top even with a chopstick. (I find the traditional dip-and-scoop method packs down a powdery ingredient as the cup pushes against it, thus making the measurement uneven.) Measure liquid and soft solid ingredients precisely in transparent measuring pitchers.

WATCH THE SPEED. Butter, eggs, and flour absorb air and other ingredients at a very particular rate, and they must be beaten at a very particular speed. Next to temperature of ingredients, I've found mixing speed the most important key to success. *Since these cakes were developed with a portable mixer, if you're working with a standard mixer, reduce speeds given in the recipe by one notch.* By the way, should butter and sugar look sandy rather than very light, or should butter, sugar, and eggs appear curdled, don't fear. Raise the speed a bit and beat until the mixture smooths out. If it doesn't, proceed with the recipe and still all will be well.

DON'T OVERBAKE. Start testing for doneness 5 to 7 minutes before the recipe indicates. A few minutes too long in the oven can dry a moist cake surprisingly. Cakes are done when a broomstraw, wooden toothpick, or bamboo or metal skewer emerges clean from the center...when they smell done...when they *start* to pull away from the sides of the pan...when the top, lightly tapped, springs back. Not every test works with every batter, so you might want to use a couple of tests. If your baking times are consistently different from the recipes', have your oven calibrated by the utility company.

SERVE FRESH. Flavor may continue developing over a day or two in a cake kept in a cool place, but the texture is always tenderest the day of baking. A cake straight from the fridge will be heavy because the butter and eggs have congealed, and sometimes, even after being brought to room temperature, the crumb never recovers its pristine form. Therefore, it's best to keep cakes in a cool (60° to 65°F) place, bringing them to room temperature before serving. Of course if the weather's hot, you have no choice but to refrigerate a cake with a butter-based frosting. Although many recommend freezing cakes, I don't. Freezing, like refrigeration, dries a delicate crumb. When I need to bake in advance, I make a cake that keeps well in a cool place. My MAKE-AHEAD NOTES at the end of each recipe tell you which cakes are appropriate for this. These notes also indicate when frostings, sauces, decorations, and other finishes may be prepared in part or completely in advance.

It's so easy...

It really is. Here are the how-to's.

CAKE PANS: Heavy aluminum or tinned steel are best. Don't use dark pans or those that are dark-coated—the cake will overbake. "Temporary" aluminum pans are all right, if you set them on a baking sheet for support.

As for size, confusion reigns. A square pan stamped "8 x 8 x 2" in fact measures 7 3/4 by 7 3/4 by 1 7/8 inches. My heavy 9-by-1 1/2-inch round cake pans (in which many of these recipes were baked) have a 7-cup capacity, while those of lighter weight hold just 6 cups—the difference lies in the diameter of the bottoms. When a pan is close to full in a recipe, I give the volume of the pan required. If yours doesn't hold that much, consult the list that follows. Don't worry if the substitute pan is a bit larger. As long as the batter fills the pan by two thirds, the cake will bake success-fully. But timing will probably be different. Don't open the oven door for the first three-quarters of the baking time called for in the recipe (the cake may fall). Start checking for doneness every 3 to 4 minutes after that.

Equivalents for Pans in this Book

♦ ONE 9-BY-1 1/2-INCH ROUND WITH A 7-CUP CAPACITY = use one 9-by-2-inch round (about 8 cups); one 9-by-2 1/2-inch springform (10 cups); one

8-by-2-inch square (actually 7 3/4-by-1 7/8-inch square, 7 cups); or, if it's appropriate, use two 8-by-1 1/2-inch rounds (5 cups each), make an additional 1/2 cup filling, and sandwich the layers together.

◆ TWO 9-BY-1 1/2-INCH ROUNDS (14 CUPS) = use two 9-by-2-inch rounds (about 8 cups each); three 8-by-1 1/2-inch rounds (4 1/2 to 5 cups each) and make an additional 1/2 cup filling; or use one 9-by-13-by-2-inch baking pan (actually 8 3/4-by-12 5/8-by-1 7/8-inches, 14 cups)—serve this in one layer or cut in half for two layers (either way, the recipe for frosting will be sufficient).

◆ THREE 9-BY-1 1/2-INCH ROUNDS (21 CUPS) = use three 9-by-2-inch rounds (about 8 cups each); three 8-by-2-inch squares (7 cups each); two 10-by-2-inch rounds (10 cups each); two 9-by-2-inch squares (10 cups each); or bake in one 9-by-13-by-2-inch pan (14 cups) and one 8-by-2-inch square (7 cups), and cut the rectangle in half to make three square layers.

◆ ONE 9-BY-2 1/2-INCH SPRINGFORM (9 CUPS) = one 9-by-3-inch springform (13 cups; the "springform" part is crucial).

◆ ONE 9-BY-13-BY-2-INCH BAKING PAN (ACTUALLY 8 3/4-BY-12 5/8-BY-1 7/8-INCHES, 14 CUPS) = essential for the butterfly, page 41; for the gingercake, page 107, use two 8-by-2-inch squares (7 cups each), fitted together and frosted as one.

◆ ONE 10-BY-2-INCH ROUND (10 CUPS) = use one 10-by-2-inch springform (10 cups); 9-by-2 1/2-inch springform pan (10 cups); or one 9-by-2-inch square (10 cups).

◆ ONE 9 1/2-BY-3 1/2-INCH BUNDT PAN (13 CUPS) = use any tube pan with 12 to 14 cups capacity.

◆ ONE 10-INCH TUBE (ACTUALLY 9 1/2-BY-4 1/4-INCH, 16 CUPS) = use any tube pan with 14 to 20 cups capacity.

PREPARING THE PANS: If you don't butter the sides of a pan, the bare metal gives the batter something to cling to on its way up, thus the batter rises to maximum height. To make turning a cake out of its pan foolproof, I line the bottom with waxed or parchment paper: First, using unsalted butter (salt makes things stick), I smear a buttery film over the bottom—that fixes the liner in place and prevents batter from gliding beneath it. Next, I butter the round of waxed paper the same way so it will easily pull away from the cake (parchment needs no buttering). I cut a stack of liners at one time, using the pan as a template. Fluted pans can't be lined, so they must be well buttered and dusted with flour or, for chocolate cakes, with cocoa.

MELTING CHOCOLATE: Chop it into 1- to 2-inch pieces and set it in a heatproof bowl over (not touching) barely simmering water (melting chocolate in the microwave takes more fussing). White and milk chocolates burn easily, so watch them closely. Do not cover and permit no steam or water to touch the chocolate or it will harden and should be replaced. Stir occasionally. When melted, turn off the heat, keeping the chocolate warm and soft. Chocolate may be remelted without harm.

ADDING THE FLOUR IN THREE PARTS ALTERNATING WITH THE LIQUID IN TWO PARTS: Use your judgment and a big kitchen spoon to sprinkle *roughly* one third the flour over the bowl each time, and slosh in roughly half the liquid. The final addition is the remaining third of the flour.

BEATING EGG WHITES: For maximum volume, beat whites just before adding them to the batter. Use scrupulously clean beaters and bowl (not plastic). Even a speck of fat keeps whites from beating to their greatest volume. When separating more than one egg, drop each white into a cup and examine it for yolk, then turn it into the bowl with the rest. Should any yolk drop into the cup, try to scoop it out with an eggshell. If there's even a trace of yolk left, start fresh.

BLENDING BEATEN EGG WHITES AND BATTER: The trick is to bring the two close to the same consistency before combining them. That's why you'll first aerate the batter by folding in one third of the whites.

FOLDING: The purpose of folding is to force air into the mixtures being blended while preserving the air that's already in them. Use great big strokes, catching the air over the bowl and sailing it down the side of the bowl, across through the contents, and up the other side. At the same time, turn the spatula in your hand slowly so it stirs like a paddle, *and* turn the bowl with your other hand so you'll reach all the batter evenly (this legerdemain soon becomes second nature).

TURNING A CAKE FROM THE PAN ONTO A COOLING RACK: You'll need two racks. Free the cake from the pan by running a table knife around the sides against the metal, not the cake. Lay a cloth over the cake, then a rack over the cloth (the cloth keeps the rack from making lines in the soft cake). Turn over, lift off the pan, remove the paper, and lay a second rack, feet up, over the cake. Again turn over, dropping the cake top side up onto the rack. Remove the cloth and cool in a draft-free place.

SPLITTING A LAYER HORIZONTALLY: Set the cake on waxed paper. (You may first want to measure the center and score it around the side with a knife as a cutting guide.) Place one hand flat on top. With a long serrated or very sharp knife, slowly cut through the center of the cake with a gentle sawing motion until halved. If you're going to be fitting the layers back together after filling them, stick a toothpick in each half, one above the other.

FROSTING NEATLY: Cover the border of the cake platter with 2- to 3-inch wide strips of waxed paper before you set the cake (or first layer) upon it. You can fill and frost with abandon. When you're finished, gently pull the strips out (the tip of a knife will hold frosting in place), revealing a spotless border.

RESCUE: Not that this will happen, but a heap of white frosting covers lopped-off corners and such on white cakes and chocolate frosting masks similar dark mistakes.

Carefree Decorating...

FLOWERS AND GREENS. Keep your decorating simple. A few robust pots of geranium, thyme, and mint in a sunny window will give you lovely decorations the year around. There's nothing more beautiful on a cake and platter than fresh flowers and leaves, but they must have been untouched by toxic chemicals. Alas, this makes most florists' offerings doubtful. Raised without toxic chemicals, all flowers and leaves suggested in this book are safe to use. The edible flowers suggested are: anise hyssop, apple blossoms, bee balm, borage flowers, calendulas, chamomile, chrysanthemums, daylilies, English daisies, geraniums, dried edible grains, fennel, hollyhocks, honeysuckle, Johnny-jump-ups, lavender, lemon blossoms, lilacs, marigolds, mustard blossoms, nasturtiums, orange blossoms, pansies, pinks, plum blossoms, roses, sage blossoms, sunflowers, thyme, tuberous begonias, tulips, violas, and violets. Suggested stalks and leaves that are *not edible* but are safe to use as decoration are unsprayed apple, grape, nasturtium, rose, and strawberry. Do not use any other flowers, stalks, or leaves without checking with your local Poison Control Center. Innocent-looking beauties can fool you.

More than flowers, decorate with colorful fruits and such amusements as candies, ribbons, and toys.

A BANNER OF GREETING. Again and again you'll read in these pages, "Plant a banner of greeting." Rather than pipe a greeting, I usually cut either a long gay pennant or a bright broad band from craft paper. With colored pens I draw the greeting on it (and usually hearts and flowers) and glue one or two sides to a chopstick or thin bamboo skewer. For formal cakes, I write simply on a large colorful card and thread it through the long stiff stem of a real or fabric rose. Then I plant the banner in the cake out of reach of candleflame. Unlike frosting, a banner makes a lasting keepsake.

BUT WHAT ABOUT PIPING? For small fast decorative touches, I push plops of frosting off the tip of a teaspoon onto the cake. You'd be surprised how pretty this spoon piping can be. Still, why not try cone piping? To make a paper cone, you'll need two 8 1/2-by-11-inch sheets of parchment paper. Holding the two sheets as one, fold one corner up to form a right angle at the center of one long side, then wrap the other corner around your hand, making a cone. Adjust until the tip is closed, then tape in place. Fill half-full with the cake's frosting or this easy Chocolate Piping (following).

Chocolate Piping

MAKES ABOUT 1/4 CUP,
ENOUGH FOR A GREETING AND A BIT OF DECORATION ON ONE CAKE

In the top of a double boiler or heatproof bowl set over barely simmering water, melt 2 ounces of dark, milk, or white chocolate (every hue of chocolate will be visible piped against every hue of frosting). If grainy, strain through a sieve. Turn into a cone, and pipe while warm. The chocolate should harden almost instantly.

Gather the top of the cone and snip the tip to make a round opening the size you wish. Practice on waxed paper: write your greeting in pencil—just as, before piping on the cake, you'll lightly write with a skewer in the frosting for a guide. Press the frosting out of the cone smoothly with one hand. If you make a mistake, lift it off with a knifetip (you can usually do this on the cake, too). You can snip the tip in 2 cuts at right angles and pipe stars. Paper cones can be used just once. If you enjoy piping, buy a cloth bag and some decorating tips, read a cake-decorating book, and press on!

For unusual ingredients and equipment, you can

ORDER BY MAIL... For European chocolate, candied flowers, and other treats: Dean & DeLuca in New York (800-221-7714). For a vast array of baking and decorating paraphernalia: Maid of Scandinavia in Minneapolis (800-328-6722). For wire whisks and an international collection of bakeware: Williams-Sonoma in San Francisco (800-541-2233). For every baking tool and toy imaginable: Bridge Kitchenware in New York (800-274-3435).

For whoso giveth a gift, or doth a grace,
Does it betimes, his thank is well the more.

—GEOFFREY CHAUCER
Prologue, *Legend of Good Women*

Chocolate for Grown-Ups

DARK CHERRIED CHOCOLATE CAKE
WITH CHERRIED CHANTILLY CREAM

*One velvety layer of the most intensely chocolate cake on the premises
(and not too sweet), with fresh cherries woven through
and perched on top of cherried French-style whipped cream.*

FRENCH CHOCOLATE CAKE
WITH CHOCOLATE TRUFFLE FROSTING

*The ultimate European chocolate cake: two thin rich dense dark
chocolate layers filled and frosted with whipped chocolate
and bordered with chocolate rags.*

MARBLED CHOCOLATE AND LEMON CAKE
WITH CHOCOLATE-SPATTERED LEMON FROSTING

*Two delicate layers of marbled buttermilk cake
tartly filled and frosted with creamy lemon, splashed with chocolate,
and decorated with lemon flowers.*

DOBOS, THE QUEEN OF TORTES

*The texture of silk and the flavor of bittersweet chocolate in
nine ultrathin vanilla sponge layers interleaved with
eight ultrathin chocolate buttercream layers, buttercream-frosted,
and finished with a caramelized sugar glaze and candied flowers.*

Dark Cherried Chocolate Cake with Cherried Chantilly Cream

Dark Cherried Chocolate Cake with Cherried Chantilly Cream

One velvety layer of the most intensely chocolate cake on the premises (and not too sweet), with fresh cherries woven through and perched on top of cherried French-style whipped cream.

"Loveliest of trees, the cherry now
Is hung with bloom along the bough..."[1]
Come summer, the boughs of our North Star
are hung with red tartly fleshed fruit. North Stars are pie cherries,
but I once stirred some into the batter of an Italian chocolate cake
and they became cake cherries, too.
As *delizioso* made with dark sweet cherries...

MAKES 10 TO 12 SERVINGS

1 pound fresh cherries, sweet or tart, for cake and cream
FOR THE PAN: *a firm lump of unsalted butter*
1/2 cup sifted cake flour
1/2 teaspoon baking soda
1/4 teaspoon salt
1/8 teaspoon pure almond extract
8 tablespoons (1 stick) unsalted butter, melted
1 cup sifted unsweetened (not Dutch process) cocoa
2/3 cup boiling water
3 extra-large eggs
3/4 cup granulated sugar
Cherried Chantilly Cream *(recipe follows)*
Handful of unsprayed rose leaves, for the decoration

TO PREPARE THE CHERRIES, leaving their stems intact, pit and reserve the handsomest 4 ounces (14 or 15) for decoration. Stem, pit, and chop the rest. Measure 1 cup for the cake, and reserve the remaining cherries for the cream.

[1]A.E. Housman, *The Shropshire Lad,* ii.

TO MAKE THE CAKE, heat the oven to 350°F. Run the lump of butter over the bottom of one 10-by-2-inch round cake pan, smooth in a round of waxed paper. Sift the flour, baking soda, and salt together. Add the almond extract to the butter. In a small heatproof bowl over barely simmering water, whisk the cocoa and water to a smooth paste, then cover and turn off the heat. Turn the eggs and sugar into a large mixing bowl and set over (not in) barely simmering water on low heat. Beat with a portable mixer on low speed until lukewarm, then turn off the heat (leaving the bowl in place) and beat on high speed until the mixture has quadrupled in volume. On low speed, blend in the cocoa. Sprinkle the flour over the batter and beat on low speed as you trickle in the butter. Add the chopped cherries and beat on low speed just until blended. Now fold the batter with a large flexible rubber spatula to finish blending thoroughly. Smooth into the pan, slightly pushing the batter up against the sides.

BAKE IN THE MIDDLE OF THE OVEN until a toothpick emerges clean from the center of the cake, 35 to 40 minutes. Cool in the pan on a rack 15 minutes, then turn out onto the rack, bottom side up, to cool completely. MAKE-AHEAD NOTE: Wrapped airtight, the untopped cake keeps fresh at room temperature for 2 days.

Cherried Chantilly Cream

MAKES 2 CUPS

   1/2 cup chopped (reserved) cherries
   1 teaspoon maraschino or kirsch liqueur (optional)
   1 cup heavy cream, chilled
   2 tablespoons sour cream, chilled (do not use a "light" substitute;
    it won't have enough body)
   About 2 tablespoons granulated sugar

To MAKE THE CREAM, combine the cherries and liqueur in a small bowl (if you're using liqueur) and set aside until needed. In a chilled bowl with chilled beaters, beat the two creams until soft peaks form. Fold in the cherries and liqueur, then add sugar to taste. MAKE-AHEAD NOTE: The creams may be beaten 4 to 5 hours in advance and refrigerated—whisk back to stiffness, should the cream slacken. Add the cherries and sugar just before using.

To ASSEMBLE THE CAKE, an hour or so before serving, set the cake on a platter. Smooth the cream over the top (leaving the sides dark in contrast). Keep on the cool side of room temperature until serving. Just before serving, arrange the (cherry-colored) candles and plant a banner of greeting. Arrange the whole cherries casually in small bunches over the top, then wreathe the bottom with leaves.

FOR AN ICE, more cherries, page 115.

My birthday began with the water-
Birds and the birds of the winged trees flying my name.
—DYLAN THOMAS
Poem in October

French Chocolate Cake with Chocolate Truffle Frosting

The ultimate European chocolate cake: two thin rich dense dark chocolate layers filled and frosted with whipped chocolate and bordered with chocolate rags.

A small bronze Degas ballerina in her own glass case in the Louvre.
Bouillabaisse on a *quai* in Marseilles, best meal of my life.
A house built into the walls of Vézélay,
where I'm sure I lived in another lifetime.
Tea and this cake on my birthday at Rumpelmayer's on the Champs Elysées...

MAKES 10 SERVINGS

FOR THE PAN: *a firm lump of unsalted butter*
2/3 cup sifted cake flour
1/2 cup unsweetened Dutch process *(European style) cocoa*
8 tablespoons (1 stick) unsalted butter, softened to the
  consistency of mayonnaise
2/3 cup granulated sugar
1/2 tablespoon pure vanilla extract
5 extra-large eggs, warmed in their shells
1/8 teaspoon salt
Chocolate Truffle Frosting *(recipe follows)*
1 ounce sweet chocolate (light color to contrast with the frosting),
  melted, for the Chocolate Rags decoration
3 tablespoons seedless raspberry preserves, for filling
Unsweetened cocoa, for dusting

TO MAKE THE CAKE, heat the oven to 300°F. Run the lump of butter over the bottom of one 9-by-1 1/2-inch round cake pan, smooth in a round of waxed paper, then butter the paper. Sift the flour and cocoa together. In a large mixing bowl, beat the butter on medium speed until creamy. Continue beating while sprinkling in 1/3 cup of the sugar a tablespoon at a time. Add the vanilla and beat until very light. Separate the eggs: Beat 5 yolks into the butter one at a time, dropping 4 of the whites into a large mixing bowl (use the extra white elsewhere). Beat until blended after each addition, then beat until very light and creamy. Add the flour in two parts (sprinkling it over the bowl)—beat on the lowest speed manageable and just until each addition disappears. Set aside. With clean beaters, beat the whites at low speed until frothy. Add the salt and beat on medium speed until soft peaks form. Beat on high speed while sprinkling in the remaining 1/3 cup sugar, a tablespoon at a time. Beat just until the peak in the bowl holds, then flops, when you lift the beaters. Add one third of the whites to the batter and blend in with a flat wire whisk or the mixer on low speed. Add the remaining whites and fold the batter with a large flexible rubber spatula to finish blending thoroughly. Smooth into the pan, slightly pushing the batter up against the sides.

BAKE IN THE MIDDLE OF THE OVEN until a toothpick emerges clean from the center of the cake, about 30 minutes. Cool in the pan on a rack 15 minutes, then turn out onto the rack, top side up, to cool completely. MAKE-AHEAD NOTE: The unsplit layer will keep fresh, wrapped airtight, at room temperature for a day or two.

Chocolate Truffle Frosting: Ganache Soufflé

MAKES ABOUT 3 1/2 CUPS

1 1/2 cups heavy cream, the freshest available
12 ounces European bittersweet chocolate (or 6 ounces each
    domestic semisweet and unsweetened or 8 ounces semisweet
    and 4 ounces unsweetened or...), coarsely chopped
1 tablespoon brandy
1 teaspoon pure vanilla extract

This is an easy frosting to make if you catch the chocolate at the point where it has thickened but not yet set. TO MAKE THE FROSTING, in a small heavy saucepan over medium-high heat, bring the cream to a boil, stirring frequently with a wooden spoon to prevent scorching. Add the chocolate, remove from the heat, stir briefly to blend, then cool 3 to 4 minutes. Now stir until all the chocolate has melted and the mixture is completely smooth. (You may need to briefly warm the mixture toward the end.) Turn into a mixing bowl and cool to room temperature: either set the bowl in a bowl of ice and stir constantly, or cover the bowl and refrigerate, checking and stirring every 4 to 5 minutes. The cream will be ready to whip when it is very thick and smooth but not yet set, much like chocolate pudding. (Should it harden, warm the cream slightly over hot water, stirring constantly, until it reaches this consistency.) Add the brandy and vanilla and beat on high speed (using a whisk attachment, if you have one) until lighter in color and roughly doubled in volume. Use at once—it sets quickly.

TO MAKE THE CHOCOLATE RAGS (these easily made waferthin ruffles and strips of pure chocolate are charming on a cake), turn the warm chocolate onto a waxed paper-lined baking sheet. Use a large flexible rubber spatula to spread the chocolate as thinly as you can without making holes. Refrigerate until firm (about 10 minutes), and keep chilled until needed. Very close to serving the cake (especially if the air is hot), invert the chocolated paper onto a second sheet of waxed paper, and pull the paper backing off the chocolate. With the pointed tip of a knife and a chopstick or a second knife, lift up the chocolate—it will become rags of its own volition. MAKE-AHEAD NOTE: the sheet of chocolate may be prepared 24 hours in advance, covered, and refrigerated.

TO ASSEMBLE THE CAKE, up to 6 hours before serving (depending upon how warm the air is), split the layer in half horizontally (page 15), setting a toothpick in each half, one above the other. Set the bottom half, cut side up, on a platter and spread with the preserves. Smooth over 1/2 cup of the frosting. Fit on the top, top side up, lining up the toothpicks. If you'll be piping a greeting, reserve about 1/4 cup of the frosting. Frost the top and sides with the rest, making dramatic swirls and curls. Pipe on the greeting or plant a banner. Keep on the cool side of room temperature until serving (if the air is warm, the chocolate will melt). Just before serving, heap the chocolate rags randomly around the border on top. Lightly sift cocoa over them and arrange the candles.

FOR AN ICE, tangy raspberries, page 115.

Cleopatra, when her fortunes had waned,
had only a modest dinner on her birthday.
But for her beloved Antony's,
she threw a party
of the utmost splendor and magnificence
worthy of her salad days.

Marbled Chocolate and Lemon Cake with Chocolate-Spattered Lemon Frosting

Two delicate layers of marbled buttermilk cake
tartly filled and frosted with creamy lemon, splashed with chocolate,
and decorated with lemon flowers.

Creamy swirls and sienna curls. Dark zingers over light.
Glints of gold and umber.
Tiffany? Pollock? Rembrandt? No, the marbling, frosting, and flavor
of this witty Italianate cake.

MAKES 10 SERVINGS

FOR THE PANS: *a firm lump of unsalted butter*
2 3/4 cups sifted cake flour
1 teaspoon baking soda
1/2 teaspoon baking powder
1/2 teaspoon salt
10 tablespoons (1 1/4 sticks) unsalted butter, softened to the
  consistency of mayonnaise
2 cups granulated sugar
4 extra-large egg whites, warmed in their shells before separating
1 3/4 cups buttermilk or soured milk, at room temperature (see NOTE*)*
Scant 1/2 teaspoon pure lemon extract
2 ounces unsweetened chocolate, melted, plus 4 ounces, melted,
  for the decoration
Pinch of cinnamon
Creamy Lemon Frosting *(recipe follows)*
1 or 2 bright lemons (Meyer, if available), for the Lemon Flowers
  decoration
NOTE: *To sour milk, place a scant 2 tablespoons fresh lemon*
juice or mild vinegar at the bottom of the measure and fill to
1 3/4 cups with sweet milk. Set in a warm place a few minutes
to clabber.

TO MAKE THE CAKE, heat the oven to 350°F. Run the lump of butter over the bottoms of two 9-by-1 1/2-inch round cake pans, smooth a round of waxed paper into each, then butter the papers. Sift the flour, baking soda, baking powder, and salt together. In a large mixing bowl, beat the butter on medium speed until creamy. Continue beating while sprinkling in the sugar a tablespoon at a time, then beat until very light. Add the egg whites one at a time, beating until blended after each, then beat until very light and creamy. Add the flour in three parts (sprinkling it over the bowl), alternating with the buttermilk in two parts—beat on the lowest speed manageable and just until each addition disappears. Now fold the batter with a large flexible rubber spatula to finish blending thoroughly. Turn half the batter into another bowl. Fold the lemon extract into one batter and 2 ounces melted chocolate and the cinnamon into the other. Divide the batters in half (half for each pan).

TO MARBLE THE BATTERS, in each pan, smooth just enough lemon batter over the bottom to cover it. Drop half the chocolate batter in spoonfuls randomly around the pan, then smooth it over the lemon with the back of a spoon. Repeat with the rest of the lemon, and then the remaining chocolate. Push the batter slightly up against the sides of the pan. Now, in the center, send the tip of a table knife straight down into the batter— just short of the bottom. Gently lift and turn the knife over, folding the batters together. Repeat every 2 inches around the pan.

BAKE BOTH PANS IN THE MIDDLE OF THE OVEN, staggering them on the rack. Bake until a toothpick emerges clean from the center of the cakes, 25 to 30 minutes. Cool in the pans on racks 15 minutes, then turn out onto the racks, top sides up, to cool completely. MAKE-AHEAD NOTE: The cake is incredibly light the day of baking, but may be wrapped airtight and kept in a cool place for a day.

Creamy Lemon Frosting

MAKES ABOUT 2 2/3 CUPS

8 tablespoons (1 stick) unsalted butter, softened
6 cups confectioners' sugar, sifted if at all lumpy
6 tablespoons fresh lemon juice
1/4 cup heavy cream, chilled

TO MAKE THE FROSTING, in a food processor or with a mixer at medium speed, cream the butter. Gradually blend in the sugar, lemon juice, and cream. Process or beat on high speed until fluffy and light (be careful not to overwork in the food processor, or it will thin out). MAKE-AHEAD NOTE: This may be prepared a day or two in advance, tightly covered, and refrigerated. If necessary, beat again until creamy before spreading.

TO MAKE THE LEMON FLOWERS, if you have a canelle knife (it makes a groove in the peel by carving out a small strip), cut about 8 grooves from stem to blossom ends in the lemons, then slice the lemons rather thin—they'll resemble flowers. Without the canelle knife, slice the lemons into paperthin rounds, then cut the rounds in half. MAKE-AHEAD NOTE: The slices will keep fresh, wrapped airtight, for a day.

To ASSEMBLE THE CAKE, up to 6 hours before serving, set the first layer, bottom side up, on a platter. Smooth over 2/3 cup of the frosting, then set on the second layer, top side up. Frost the top and sides of the cake. When the frosting has set, while someone holds and tips the platter, dip a fork into the remaining 4 ounces melted chocolate and splash and snap and swizzle it over the sides, then the top. Keep on the cool side of room temperature until serving. Just before serving, plant a banner of greeting (a piped greeting would be lost). Make a sunny border of lemon flowers or overlap the halves of lemon slices around the platter, round sides out. Arrange the (lemon-colored) candles.

FOR AN ICE, Meyer lemon—or, for a Meyer lemon flavor, lemon-with-orange, page 116.

*All admit that in a certain sense
the several kinds of character
are bestowed by nature.
Justice, a tendency to Temperance,
Courage, and the other types of character
are exhibited from the moment of birth.*

—ARISTOTLE

Nicomachean Ethics

Dobos, The Queen of Tortes

*The texture of silk and the flavor of bittersweet chocolate in
nine ultrathin vanilla sponge layers interleaved with
eight ultrathin chocolate buttercream layers, buttercream-frosted,
and finished with a caramelized sugar glaze and candied flowers.*

Hoping to make something spectacular for my husband's birthday,
I baked an exciting-sounding cake from a European cookbook.
When I finished, the layers looked like a stack of floppy pancakes.
I was about to throw them out when a Viennese friend came by.
"Sylvia," she exclaimed, "a Dobos Torte!" They were *supposed* to look like that!
It was the most fabulous cake we've ever tasted, and
I still make it each year for his birthday.

MAKES 12 SERVINGS

CHOCOLATE FOR GROWN-UPS

FOR THE PANS: *a firm lump of unsalted butter*
5 extra-large eggs, warmed in their shells
1/2 cup granulated sugar, plus 1/2 cup for the glaze
1/2 tablespoon pure vanilla extract
Pinch of salt
1/2 cup sifted cake flour
Bittersweet Chocolate Buttercream *(recipe follows)*
Candied Flowers *for the decoration (recipe follows)*

The assembled torte must have 12 to 24 hours ripening time. TO MAKE
THE CAKE LAYERS, heat the oven to 375°F. Run the lump of butter over
the bottoms of as many round 8-inch cake pans as you have. (The best
thing is to borrow what you need, so you can distribute the batter evenly
among nine pans. The batter won't suffer from waiting for its turn in the
oven.) Smooth a round of waxed paper into each pan, then generously
butter the papers. Separate the eggs into 2 large mixing bowls. Beat the
yolks on medium speed until pale. Continue beating while adding 1/4 cup
of the sugar a tablespoon at a time. Add the vanilla, then beat until thick
and mousselike. Now with clean beaters, beat the whites at low speed
until frothy. Add the salt and beat at medium speed until soft peaks form,
then beat on high speed while sprinkling in the remaining 1/4 cup
sugar, a tablespoon at a time. Beat just until the peak in the bowl holds,
then flops, when you lift the beaters. Sprinkle the flour over the batter
(do not mix), then add one third of the whites. Blend in with a flat whisk
or the mixer on low speed. Add the remaining whites and fold into the
batter with a large flexible rubber spatula to finish blending thoroughly.
Working swiftly, turn a rounded 1/3 cup of the batter into each pan. Use
the bottom of a broad spoon to smooth the batter, pushing it slightly up
against the sides of the pan.

BAKE 2 LAYERS ON THE MIDDLE RACK AND 2 ON THE LOWER RACK OF THE
OVEN—stagger them so the top layers are not directly above the bottom
ones. Bake just until a toothpick emerges clean from the center of the cake,
5 to 8 minutes. Turn out onto racks to cool (use a toaster oven rack and
whatever other racks you can find), leaving the waxed papers in place.
Bake the remaining layers. If necessary, prepare and fill the pans as before.
MAKE-AHEAD NOTE: Although the layers may be cooled, interleaved with

plastic film, wrapped airtight, and refrigerated a day or two, some of the delicate cake will stick to the film when you separate them, so unless you're terribly pressed, best not to do this.

Bittersweet Chocolate Buttercream

MAKES ABOUT 4 1/3 CUPS

4 ounces domestic unsweetened and 3 ounces domestic semisweet
    chocolate, or 7 ounces European bittersweet chocolate, coarsely
    chopped (see NOTE)
3 1/2 tablespoons very hot coffee
7 extra-large eggs
3/4 cup plus 2 tablespoons granulated sugar
24 tablespoons (3 sticks) unsalted butter, softened to the
    consistency of mayonnaise
2 teaspoons pure vanilla extract
NOTE: *Although some people prefer the flavor of Swiss chocolate
here, I've found the resulting buttercream can be unpredictably
thinner—thus the torte doesn't stand as tall—and paler—thus the
contrast between layers isn't as dramatic.*

TO MAKE THE BUTTERCREAM, in a heatproof bowl over barely simmering water, melt both chocolates with the coffee. Turn off the heat, cover and keep warm. In a large mixing bowl over simmering water, beat the eggs and sugar at medium speed just until the eggs thicken and coat a wooden spoon. Remove from the water and cover. In a small mixing bowl, beat the butter on high speed until pale, then slowly beat in the melted chocolate and the vanilla. On lowest manageable speed, beat the butter mixture into the eggs. Set in a cool place until ready to use. MAKE-AHEAD NOTE: The buttercream may be prepared, covered airtight, and refrigerated a day or two. Bring to room temperature before spreading.

Candied Flowers

Granulated sugar
1 egg white
1 teaspoon cool water
12 unsprayed violets, Johnny-jump-ups, violas, pansies,
* honeysuckle, plum, lemon or orange blossoms, or any small*
* flowers or petals of large flowers suggested on page 16*

TO CANDY THE FLOWERS, cover a tray with sugar. In a small bowl, beat the egg white and water with a fork until frothy and the white has loosened. With a delicate brush, paint the petals on both sides with a veil of the mixture, then sprinkle over just enough sugar to sparkle but not so much that you can't see the color beneath. Dry the flowers on the tray in a cool place, an hour or two or three. MAKE-AHEAD NOTE: For brightest colors, use within a few hours. The flowers will keep in a tightly covered jar for months.

TO ASSEMBLE THE TORTE, set aside the handsomest layer for the top. Place the thickest layer on (a fabric doily on) a platter, bottom side up, removing the paper. Smooth a rounded 1/4 cup (5 tablespoons) of buttercream over the layer. Neatly stack and fill the remaining layers the same way, compensating for any unevenness in the layers with frosting—a little more here, a little less there—so the final layer will lie flat. Place the reserved layer, bottom side up, on top.

TO MAKE THE GLAZE, in a small heavy skillet over medium heat, melt the remaining 1/3 cup sugar, stirring constantly with a wooden spoon. Turn heat to low and swirl the pan gently (don't stir) until the sugar browns to the color of hazelnuts—it can be almost the moment after melting. Remove from the heat. *At no time touch the hot glaze with your fingers.*

Working fastfastfast—it sets within a minute—pour the glaze evenly over the top of the torte and smooth with a knife to the edges. Reserving 1/3 to 1/2 cup of the remaining buttercream for decoration, swirl the rest over the sides. Pipe or dollop a decorative connection between the rough edges of the glaze and the smooth buttercream on the sides. Pipe or spoon dots of buttercream for candle bases. If you choose, pipe the greeting on top, and pipe or spoon a border around the base of the torte. Without covering (it melts the glaze), set the torte in a cold place (not the refrigerator unless you have no other cold place) for 12 to 24 hours to ripen. Before serving, place 12 candied flowers evenly around the edge (they'll be in the center of each slice). Set in the candles, and, if you're using one, tuck a banner of greeting on a slender bamboo stick in the center. Slice with a thin serrated knife—the caramel will have softened enough to cut.

AN ICE would be superfluous. (By the way, Hungarians, and those on intimate terms with the torte, pronounce it DOBOSCH.)

In earliest times,
until the christening ceremony,
a baby's name was kept secret
from all but the parents,
lest a fairy seize the name and
use it to cast a spell on the child.
In some cultures today, a name is still thought so powerful,
it may never be spoken, and even wives and husbands
must call their beloved by a false name, given at birth.

A Birthday

My heart is like a singing bird
    Whose nest is in a water'd shoot;
My heart is like an apple-tree
    Whose boughs are bent with thickset fruit;
My heart is like a rainbow shell
    That paddles in a halcyon sea;
My heart is gladder than all these,
    Because my love is come to me.

Raise me a daïs of silk and down;
    Hang it with vair and purple dyes;
Carve it in doves and pomegranates,
    And peacocks with a hundred eyes;
Work it in gold and silver grapes,
    In leaves and silver fleurs-de-lys;
Because the birthday of my life
    Is come, my love is come to me.

        —Christina Georgina Rossetti

Especially for kids

A CHILD'S GOLDEN BUTTERFLY
OF ORANGE CAKE WITH
MERINGUE-MARMALADE-AND-JAM FROSTING

A simple butterfly cut from a rectangle of light orange buttermilk cake, with billowy sunset pink frosting, wings decorated with colorful fruits, and flower antennae.

FUDGY-BROWNIE-STRAWBERRY-ICE-CREAM-
CHOCOLATE-WHIPPED-CREAM CAKE!

Four thin layers of moist chocolate cake spread with strawberry jam, filled with three layers of strawberry ice cream, and swathed in chocolate whipped cream with chocolate jimmies.

PEANUT BUTTER CAKE
WITH SCRUMPTIOUS
CHOCOLATE-PEANUT BUTTER FROSTING

Two feathery peanut-buttery layers filled and frosted with sensational chocolate-peanut butter frosting and set with chocolate stars.

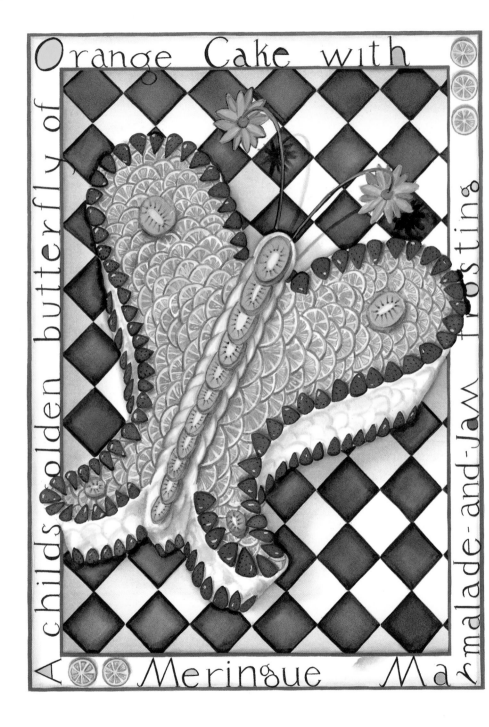

Orange Cake with Meringue Marmalade-and-Jam Frosting

A childs golden butterfly of

A Child's Golden Butterfly of Orange Cake with Meringue-Marmalade-and-Jam Frosting

*A simple butterfly cut from a rectangle of light orange
buttermilk cake, with billowy sunset pink frosting,
wings decorated with colorful fruits, and flower antennae.*

I find children's parties fiendish. Children are not only unpredictable,
they have no social grace. I once spent a day making a chocolate horse cake
(coffee-can body, kaiser-roll head, peppermint-stick legs)
for our firstborn and his 3-year-old friends. But at the party,
not a word was said about my horse. So even if the darlings
don't mention your butterfly, at least they'll want seconds of your cake.

MAKES 12 TO 20 SERVINGS

FOR THE PAN: *a firm lump of unsalted butter*
2 cups sifted cake flour
1 teaspoon baking powder
1/2 teaspoon baking soda
1/2 teaspoon salt
*8 tablespoons (1 stick) unsalted butter, softened to the
consistency of mayonnaise*
1 1/4 cups granulated sugar
1 teaspoon pure vanilla extract
2 extra-large eggs, warmed in their shells
*3/4 cup plus 2 tablespoons (7 fluid ounces) buttermilk or soured
milk, at room temperature (see* NOTE*)*
2 tablespoons finely grated orange or tangerine zest
Meringue-Marmalade-and-Jam Frosting *(recipe follows)*
*Slices of strawberries, kiwis, grapes (green and purple), and all
sorts of bright fresh fruit, for the decoration*
*2 smallish brightly-colored perky unsprayed flowers such as
calendulas, English daisies, or button chrysanthemums (in a*

pinch, use furls of parsley) with 3-inch-long stems, for the antennae
NOTE: *To sour milk, place a scant 1 tablespoon fresh lemon juice or mild vinegar at the bottom of the measure and fill to 7 fluid ounces with sweet milk. Set in a warm place a few minutes to clabber.*

TO MAKE THE CAKE, heat the oven to 350°F. Run the lump of butter over the bottom of one 9-by-13-by-2-inch cake pan, smooth in a rectangle of waxed paper, then butter the paper. Sift the flour, baking powder, baking soda, and salt together. In a large mixing bowl, beat the butter on medium speed until creamy. Continue beating while sprinkling in the sugar a tablespoon at a time. Add the vanilla and beat until very light. Add the eggs, one at a time, beating until blended after each, then beat until very light and creamy. Add the flour in three parts (sprinkling it over the bowl), alternating with the buttermilk in two parts—beat on the lowest speed manageable and just until each addition disappears. Sprinkle over the orange zest and fold the batter with a large flexible rubber spatula to finish blending thoroughly. Smooth into the pan, slightly pushing the batter up against the sides.

BAKE IN THE MIDDLE OF THE OVEN until a toothpick emerges clean from the center of the cake, about 30 minutes. Cool in the pan on a rack 15 minutes, then turn out onto the rack, top side up, to cool completely. MAKE-AHEAD NOTE: Best the day of baking, the cake may be wrapped airtight and kept in a cool place for a day before metamorphosing. NOTE: The enchanting butterfly on the previous page is curvier than the simple one you'll make, which is drawn below. To round the wings, trim the corners, if you like.

TO FREE THE BUTTERFLY FROM THE RECTANGLE (these directions take longer to read than to do), cut a strip 2 inches wide from a short side of the cake: this is the body. Center it the long way on your serving tray (which should be at least 13 by 15 1/2 inches). Next, cut the cake from corner to corner in an "X," creating four wing pieces. The blocky triangles with edges on the short sides of the cake are lower wings: set them on either side of the body, with two sides making a straight line at a right angle to the body. The remaining triangles are upper wings: set one on either side of the body above the lower two—angle these wings up slightly, like raised arms. Now make the frosting.

Meringue-Marmalade-and-jam Frosting

MAKES ABOUT 6 CUPS

1 cup sweet orange marmalade
1/2 cup seedless blackberry jam (see NOTE)
1/2 cup (about 3 extra-large) egg whites, warmed in their shells
     before separating
NOTE: This makes a sunset pink frosting with sparkling flavor,
but do experiment with other jams.

TO MAKE THE FROSTING, in the top of a double boiler or heatproof bowl set over simmering water, beat the marmalade, jam, and egg whites at high speed until the whites are cooked and the meringue holds its shape when the beaters are lifted, 10 to 12 minutes—scrape down the bowl frequently as you beat. Use at once.

TO ASSEMBLE THE BUTTERFLY, up to 2 hours before serving (depending upon how warm the air is), cover each piece of cake with frosting, then return to its place. Keep on the cool side of room temperature until serving. As close to serving time as possible, arrange fruit on the wings in patterns that might resemble a butterfly's. Tuck the flower antennae into the top of the cake rather than down low by the tray. Set candles down the center of the body. Lay a colorful card with the greeting on the tray.

FOR AN ICE, bright strawberry, page 115.

Fudgy Brownie-Strawberry Ice-Cream-Chocolate Whipped Cream Cake!

Four thin layers of moist chocolate cake spread with strawberry jam, filled with three layers of strawberry ice cream, and swathed in chocolate whipped cream with chocolate jimmies.

When I was a little girl, Jill Klein's mother always gave her a magnificent mountain of ice cream-whipped cream cake for her birthday. My mother always gave me uggy things like mocha torte and rocky road ice cream. To save your little ones from such a fate, make them this cloud of a daydream.

MAKES 12 TO 14 GENEROUS SERVINGS
(OR USE THE TWO LAYERS UNSPLIT AND SERVE 8 TO 10)

ESPECIALLY FOR KIDS

FOR THE PANS: *a firm lump of unsalted butter*
2 1/4 cups sifted cake flour
1 1/4 teaspoons baking soda
1/2 teaspoon salt
2/3 cup sifted unsweetened (not Dutch-processed) cocoa
1 cup boiling water
16 tablespoons (2 sticks) unsalted butter, softened to the
  consistency of mayonnaise
3/4 cup granulated sugar
3/4 cup (firmly packed) light brown sugar, lumps crushed
2 teaspoons pure vanilla extract
2 extra-large eggs, warmed in their shells
1/2 cup buttermilk or soured milk, at room temperature (see NOTE)
1/2 gallon strawberry (or the birthday person's favorite) ice
  cream, softened
Chocolate Whipped Cream *(recipe follows)*
3/4 cup strawberry jam (seedless blackberry or raspberry for older
  children?), for the filling
About 2 tablespoons chocolate jimmies, for the decoration
NOTE: *To sour milk, place 1/2 tablespoon fresh lemon juice or
mild vinegar at the bottom of the measure and fill to 1/2 cup with
sweet milk. Set in a warm place a few minutes to clabber.*

TO MAKE THE CAKE, heat the oven to 350°F. Run the lump of butter over
the bottoms of two 9-by-1 1/2-inch round cake pans, smooth a round of
waxed paper into each, then butter the papers. Sift the flour, baking
soda, and salt together. In a small bowl over barely simmering water,
whisk the cocoa and boiling water to a smooth paste, then cover and
turn off the heat. In a large mixing bowl, beat the butter on medium
speed until creamy. Continue beating while sprinkling in the granulated
and brown sugars a tablespoonful at a time. Add the vanilla and beat
until very light. Add the eggs, one at a time, beating until blended after
each, then beat until very light and creamy. Blend in half the flour (sprinkling
it over the bowl), then the cocoa, the remaining flour, then the buttermilk—
beat on the lowest manageable speed, and just until each addition
disappears. Now fold the batter with a large flexible rubber spatula to finish

blending thoroughly. Divide the batter between the pans, smoothing the tops, and slightly pushing the batter up against the sides.

BAKE BOTH PANS IN THE MIDDLE OF THE OVEN, staggering them on the rack. Bake until a toothpick emerges clean from the center of the cakes, about 30 minutes. Cool in the pans on racks 15 minutes, then turn out onto the racks, top sides up, to cool completely. MAKE-AHEAD NOTE: Best the day of baking, the cake may be wrapped airtight and kept in a cool place for a day.

TO MOLD THE ICE CREAM, line three 9-inch cake pans with foil, divide the ice cream equally among them, and smooth the tops. Wrap and freeze up to 48 hours.

Chocolate Whipped Cream

MAKES 4 CUPS

2 cups heavy cream, chilled
3 tablespoons granulated sugar
1/4 cup unsifted unsweetened cocoa (any sort)
1/2 tablespoon pure vanilla extract

TO MAKE THE WHIPPED CREAM, place the cream, sugar, cocoa, and vanilla in a large mixing bowl and chill with the beaters 1 hour. (If pressed for time, chill all but the cocoa as long as possible, then sift in the cocoa before beating.) Beat until stiff enough to spread. Use at once.

TO ASSEMBLE THE CAKE, split the cake layers in half horizontally (page 15). On a flat surface, lay three of the cake layers, split sides up. Spread each with jam, just enough to cover the layer. Set the thickest layer, jam side up, on a foil-covered round of cardboard or a freezable platter. Press an unmolded layer of ice cream gently on top. Continue layering the same way with the remaining cake and ice cream, then set the last cake layer on, top side up. Frost all over with the Chocolate Whipped Cream, sprinkle with chocolate jimmies, then freeze, uncovered. When firm, wrap airtight in plastic film, then heavy foil. You can either serve the cake straight from the freezer (it's tasty frozen), or remove it and leave at room temperature about 15 minutes before serving. Plant a banner of greeting and arrange the candles. MAKE-AHEAD NOTE: *Very* well wrapped, the assembled cake may be kept in the freezer up to one week.

In many parts of the world,
it is traditional to give the birthday child
spanks and pinches
or to pour water on him—
these curious customs were once thought
to encourage growth and fertility.

Peanut Butter Cake with Scrumptious Chocolate-Peanut Butter Frosting

Two feathery peanut-buttery layers filled and frosted with sensational chocolate-peanut butter frosting and set with chocolate stars.

Do you also live with someone who, when deep in the icebox, mumbles something about looking for an apple, when in fact he's snitching from the peanut butter jar?
And is that person the same who knows nothing about The Disappearing Chocolate? Then what can we do but bake them this chocolatey peanut butter bliss for their birthdays?

MAKES 10 TO 12 SERVINGS

FOR THE PANS: *a firm lump of unsalted butter*
2 1/4 cups sifted cake flour
2 teaspoons baking powder
1 teaspoon salt
4 tablespoons (1/2 stick) unsalted butter, softened to the
  consistency of mayonnaise
1 1/2 cups granulated sugar
1/2 tablespoon pure vanilla extract
3 extra-large eggs, warmed in their shells
2/3 cup smooth-style peanut butter (and this is important)
  without sugar, salt, or additives, at room temperature
1 cup plus 2 tablespoons whole milk, at room temperature
Scrumptious Chocolate-Peanut Butter Frosting *(recipe follows)*
5 ounces sweet or semisweet chocolate, melted, for the Chocolate
  Stars *decoration*
Chocolate Piping, *page 17 (optional)*

TO MAKE THE CAKE, heat the oven to 375°F. Run the lump of butter over
the bottoms of two 9-by-1 1/2-inch round cake pans, smooth in a round
of waxed paper, then butter the papers. Sift the flour, baking powder, and
salt together. In a large mixing bowl, beat the butter on medium speed until
creamy. Continue beating while sprinkling in the sugar a tablespoon at a
time. Add the vanilla, then beat until very light. Add the eggs, one at a
time, beating until blended after each, then beat until very light and creamy.
Add the peanut butter and blend thoroughly. Add the flour in three parts
(sprinkling it over the bowl), alternating with the milk in two parts—beat
on the lowest manageable speed and just until each addition disappears.
Now fold the batter with a large flexible rubber spatula to finish blending
thoroughly. Divide the batter between the pans, smoothing the tops, and
slightly pushing the batter up against the sides.

BAKE BOTH PANS IN THE MIDDLE OF THE OVEN, staggering them on the rack.
Bake until a toothpick inserted in the center of the cakes emerges clean,
about 30 minutes. Cool in the pans on racks 15 minutes, then turn out
onto the racks, top sides up, to cool completely. MAKE-AHEAD NOTE: Serve
this cake the day of baking.

Scrumptious Chocolate Peanut Butter Frosting

MAKES ABOUT 2 1/2 CUPS

1/2 cup plus 1 tablespoon unsweetened unsalted smooth-style
   peanut butter
5 tablespoons (scant 2/3 stick) unsalted butter, softened
3 1/3 cups confectioners' sugar, sifted if at all lumpy
1/2 cup plus 1 tablespoon unsweetened (not Dutch process) cocoa
1/2 cup plus 1 tablespoon half-and-half
1/2 tablespoon pure vanilla extract
Scant 1/4 teaspoon salt

To MAKE THE FROSTING, in a food processor or with a mixer at medium speed, cream the peanut butter and butter. Gradually blend in the sugar, cocoa, half-and-half, vanilla, and salt. Process or beat until fluffy and light (do not overwork in the food processor, or it will thin out). MAKE-AHEAD NOTE: This may be prepared a day or two in advance, tightly wrapped, and refrigerated.

To MAKE THE CHOCOLATE STARS (OR HEARTS OR BEARS), on a waxed paper-lined baking sheet, smooth the chocolate into roughly a 12-inch square. Chill until the chocolate just begins to set. Cut out all the stars you can with a 1 1/2- to 2-inch star-shaped (or any-shaped) cookie cutter—this

ESPECIALLY FOR KIDS

makes at least 30 figures. Chill until the chocolate sets completely, then peel away the paper and lift up the cut-outs, handling them as little as possible. Layer between waxed paper in a tightly covered container and keep in a cool place. MAKE-AHEAD NOTE: They'll keep 1 year. Sure they will.

TO ASSEMBLE THE CAKE, up to 6 hours before serving, set the thickest layer, bottom side up, on a platter. Smooth over 2/3 cup of the frosting, then set on the second layer, top side up. Frost the top and sides of the cake and pipe a greeting, if you choose to. Keep on the cool side of room temperature until serving. Just before serving, plant a banner of greeting (if you're using one), arrange the candles near the center of the cake, and stand 10 or 12 (the number of servings) chocolate cut-outs facing outward around the edge of the cake. Press 10 or 12 more against the sides of the cake around the bottom.

FOR AN ICE, what's peanut butter without grape! Make it fresh, page 115.

Children's birthday parties, as we know them,
began in Germany around the end of the eighteenth century.
German-born Queen Victoria
introduced the custom to England,
giving a constant round of parties
for her nine children.

Classics With a Difference

APPLE/PEAR-WALNUT/HAZELNUT CAKE
WITH LEMONY PASTRY CREAM AND
A MOSAIC OF GLAZED FRESH FRUIT

*One tall dark layer moist with fresh apples or pears,
spicy with cardamom and walnuts or filberts,
bejeweled with fruits over pastry cream.*

OLD WORLD CARROT CAKE
WITH SOUR CREAM CHEESE FROSTING

*One tall layer of uncommonly light (not oily) carrot cake with
a crunchy cover of toasted walnuts and
a refreshingly unsweet creamy frosting.*

LEMON CHEESECAKE
IN A GINGERSNAP-PECAN CRUST,
CROWNED WITH
A SUNBURST OF BURGUNDY-POACHED PEAR SLICES

*Luscious New York-style cheesecake with a California finish—
connoisseurs have called it the best they've ever eaten.*

APPLE / PEAR WALNUT / HAZELNUT CAKE WITH LEMONY PASTRY CREAM AND A MOSAIC OF GLAZED FRESH FRUIT

Apple/Pear-Walnut/Hazelnut Cake with Lemony Pastry Cream and a Mosaic of Glazed Fresh Fruit

One tall dark layer moist with fresh apples or pears,
spicy with cardamom and walnuts or hazelnuts,
bejeweled with fruits over pastry cream.

A heavenly cake for a country mouse with cosmopolitan sensibilities.
Or for a cosmopolitan mouse with a country mouse's.
(For a Gemini like me...)

MAKES 14 SERVINGS

FOR THE PAN: *a firm lump of unsalted butter*
2 cups sifted cake flour
1 1/8 teaspoons baking powder
1 1/8 teaspoons baking soda
2 1/2 teaspoons ground cardamom (if unavailable, use 1 teaspoon
   cinnamon and 1 teaspoon mace)
1/2 teaspoon salt
1 cup (about 4 ounces) chopped toasted walnuts or hazelnuts
1/2 cup (about 2 ounces) seeded muscat or other large dark raisins
8 tablespoons (1 stick) unsalted butter, softened to the
   consistency of mayonnaise
1 cup (firmly packed) light brown sugar, lumps crushed
2 teaspoons pure vanilla extract
3 extra-large eggs, warmed in their shells
2 cups finely chopped unpeeled but cored fresh ripe apples or
   pears (2 large); chop at the last moment—the food processor is
   ideal for this
Lemony Pastry Cream *(recipe follows)*

Jelly Glaze *(recipe follows)*
2 to 3 cups of the most colorful and handsome assortment of fresh fruits available—peeled and pitted, sliced and diced into generous-sized pieces that are close to the same height (anything that would be appealing in a tart); premium-quality canned or frozen fruit very closely resembling fresh might be considered in wintertime

TO MAKE THE CAKE, heat the oven to 350°F. Run the lump of butter over the bottom of one 10-by-2-inch round cake pan, smooth in a round of waxed paper, then butter the paper. Sift the flour, baking powder, baking soda, cardamom, and salt together. In a bowl, mix the nuts and raisins, separating the raisins if stuck. In a large mixing bowl, beat the butter on medium speed until creamy. Continue beating while sprinkling in the brown sugar a tablespoon at a time. Add the vanilla and beat until very light. Add the eggs, one at a time, beating until blended after each, then beat until very light and creamy. Add the flour in three parts (sprinkling it over the bowl), alternating with the apples or pears in two parts—beat on the lowest manageable speed and just until each addition disappears. Sprinkle the nuts and raisins over the bowl, then fold the batter with a large flexible rubber spatula to finish blending thoroughly. Smooth into the pan, slightly pushing the batter up against the sides.

BAKE IN THE MIDDLE OF THE OVEN until a toothpick emerges clean from the center of the cake, 40 to 45 minutes. Cool in the pan on a rack 15 minutes, then turn out onto the rack, top side up, to cool completely. MAKE-AHEAD NOTE: The cake may be baked, wrapped airtight, and kept at room temperature for a day before serving.

Lemony Pastry Cream

MAKES ABOUT 1 CUP

2 extra-large egg yolks
3 tablespoons granulated sugar
2 1/2 teaspoons all-purpose flour
Tiniest pinch of salt
3/4 cup whole milk
Finely grated zest of 1 small lemon
1 tablespoon fresh lemon juice

TO MAKE THE PASTRY CREAM, turn the yolks into a small mixing bowl. In another, blend the sugar, flour, and salt. Heat the milk in a small heavy saucepan over medium heat until bubbles form around the edge. Whisk while drizzling about half the hot milk into the sugar mixture, then whisk this mixture back into the pot. Return to the heat and whisk continually while the cream comes to a boil, then boils 1 minute. Whisk a little of the cream into the yolks, then whisk this mixture back into the pot. Return to lowest heat and whisk while the cream cooks 1 minute. Pass through a sieve into a bowl, then stir in the lemon zest and juice. Smooth plastic film over the top (so a skin won't form) and chill. Whisk again before using. MAKE-AHEAD NOTE: This will keep fresh, covered airtight, 2 to 3 days in the refrigerator.

Jelly Glaze

MAKES A SCANT 1/2 CUP

6 tablespoons best-quality golden jelly, such as apple or quince; if the fruits to be glazed are predominantly red, use red currant or strawberry

1 1/2 tablespoons compatible fruit liqueur or strained fruit juice, or water

TO MAKE THE GLAZE, over low heat or at half power in the microwave, melt the jelly with the liquid, stirring until smooth. MAKE-AHEAD NOTE: The glaze may be prepared several days in advance, covered and refrigerated, then warmed.

TO ASSEMBLE THE CAKE, up to 2 hours before serving, set the cake on a platter, right side up. Smooth the pastry cream over the top (the sides stay bare). Beginning at the edge, arrange the fruit in circles—or in any pattern you please—setting the pieces so closely that you can barely see the cream. When the arrangement is complete, use a teaspoon or pastry brush to merely moisten each piece of fruit with warm glaze so the fruit sparkles. Before the glaze sets, tuck in the candles (the color of the palest fruit) and plant a banner of greeting. Keep on the cool side of room temperature until serving.

FOR AN ICE, to underscore the heart of the cake, apple or pear, page 116.

In some European cultures,
trees are planted to celebrate a child's birth—
an apple tree for a boy, a pear tree for a girl—
and as the tree prospers,
so will the child...

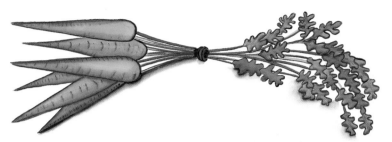

OLd World Carrot Cake
with Sour Cream Cheese Frosting

*One tall layer of uncommonly light (not oily) carrot cake with
a crunchy cover of toasted walnuts and
a refreshingly unsweet creamy frosting.*

At Berkeley, after classes, we had coffee at the Old World Café.
Dim and cozy, we felt we were in the Vienna of innocent days.
Had carrot cake been invented then, it would have been perfect there.
One of the great notions, carrot cake, earthy yet refined.
This one is special, and especially for old friends.

MAKES 10 TO 12 SERVINGS

FOR THE PAN: *a firm lump of unsalted butter*
1 1/3 cups all-purpose flour, lightly spooned into the cup
3/4 teaspoon baking powder
3/4 teaspoon baking soda
1/2 teaspoon salt
1/2 tablespoon cinnamon
1/2 teaspoon nutmeg
1/2 teaspoon ground cloves
2 cups (firmly packed) finely shredded unpeeled carrots (about 3
    large)
2/3 cup canned crushed pineapple, squeezed of juice (most of one
    15 to 20-ounce can)
1/2 cup seeded muscat or other large dark raisins, plumped if not

soft in the pineapple juice
3 extra-large eggs, warmed in their shells
1 cup granulated sugar
2/3 cup walnut oil (or 1/3 cup walnut and 1/3 cup canola or
    safflower, or 2/3 cup either of these oils)
1/2 tablespoon pure vanilla extract
1 cup coarsely chopped walnuts
Sour Cream Cheese Frosting *(recipe follows)*
About 4 yards 1 1/4-inch wide-carrot-colored fabric ribbon made
    into 8 fat bows, for the decoration

TO MAKE THE CAKE, heat the oven to 350°F. Run the lump of butter over the bottom of one 9-inch round cake pan with a 7-cup capacity (equivalent pans are listed on page 2). Smooth in a round of waxed paper, then butter the paper. Sift the flour, baking powder, baking soda, salt, cinnamon, nutmeg, and cloves together. In a bowl, mix the carrots, pineapple, and raisins, separating the raisins if stuck. In a large mixing bowl, beat the eggs on medium speed until blended, then continue beating while sprinkling in the sugar a tablespoon at a time. Continue beating while drizzling in the oil and vanilla, then beat until very thick. Blend in the flour in two parts (sprinkling it over the bowl)—beat on the lowest manageable speed, and just until each addition disappears. Sprinkle the carrot mixture over the bowl, then fold the batter with a large flexible rubber spatula to finish blending thoroughly. Smooth into the pan, slightly pushing the batter up against the sides. Sprinkle the walnuts evenly over the top.

BAKE IN THE MIDDLE OF THE OVEN until a toothpick emerges clean from the center of the cake, about 45 minutes. Cool in the pan on a rack 15 minutes, then turn out onto the rack, top side up, to cool completely (return any dislodged nuts to the top). MAKE-AHEAD NOTE: Well wrapped and stored in a cool place (not the refrigerator), the unfrosted cake keeps fresh 2 to 3 days.

Sour Cream Cheese Frosting

MAKES A GENEROUS 2 CUPS

1 cup (8 ounces—low-fat is fine) cream cheese, broken into bits
and softened

8 tablespoons (1 stick) unsalted butter, softened
1 cup confectioners' sugar, sifted if at all lumpy
1 teaspoon pure vanilla extract
2/3 cup sour cream (do not use a "light" substitute; it won't have
enough body)

TO MAKE THE FROSTING, in a food processor, blender, or mixing bowl, blend the cream cheese and butter until smooth. Slowly blend in the sugar, then the vanilla. When smooth, add the sour cream and beat just enough to blend it in. Do not overwork in the food processor or blender, or it will thin out. MAKE-AHEAD NOTE: The frosting keeps well, tightly covered, in the refrigerator for a day or two.

TO ASSEMBLE THE CAKE, up to 2 hours before serving, set the cake on a platter. Without jostling the nuts, smooth the frosting over the top and sides. Keep on the cool side of room temperature until serving. Just before serving, set the bows on the platter around the cake, plant a banner of greeting, and arrange the (carrot-colored) candles.

FOR AN ICE, the richness of continental-roast coffee, page 117.

The custom of lighted candles on cakes
is said to have started in ancient Greece.
Later, in medieval Germany,
candles again appeared on celebratory cakes—
one for each year,
plus one for the year to come.
Birthday candles were considered magic.
In time, children made wishes over the candles,
then blew the candles out.
If the child failed to blow out all the candles in one puff,
it was feared the magic of their light—
and the wish—
would fail.

CLASSICS WITH A DIFFERENCE

Lemon Cheesecake in a Gingersnap-Pecan Crust crowned with a Sunburst of Burgundy-Poached Pear Slices

Luscious New York-style cheesecake with a California finish—
connoisseurs have called it the best they've ever eaten.

Some couples have a song that brings back memories of the night they met.
My husband and I have burgundy-poached pears with sour cream.
Cheesecake has another memory for us, so I combined the two.
Ripely sensuous and beautiful, make this for someone in love.

MAKES 14 SERVINGS

Gingersnap-Pecan Crust

FOR THE PAN: *1 tablespoon soft unsalted butter*
2 cups gingersnap crumbs (grind the cookies in a food processor or
*   blender, or crush between sheets of waxed paper with a rolling pin)*
1 cup ground toasted pecans
2 tablespoons granulated sugar
1 teaspoon cinnamon
8 tablespoons (1 stick) unsalted butter, melted

TO PREPARE CRUST, heat the oven to 350°F. Brush the bottom of one 9-by-
2- or 2 1/2-inch springform cake pan generously with butter. In a mixing
bowl, stir with a fork to blend the crumbs and nuts, then blend in the
sugar, cinnamon, and butter. With the fork, press the crumbs evenly
over the bottom of the pan. Bake in the middle of the oven 10 minutes,
then cool on a rack. MAKE-AHEAD NOTE: The crust may be prepared to this
point the day before filling and baking. Keep in a cool place.

Lemon Cheesecake

FOR THE PAN: *about 1 tablespoon soft unsalted butter*
16 ounces cream cheese (low-fat is fine), at room temperature
3/4 cup granulated sugar
4 extra-large eggs, warmed in their shells
1/2 cup sour cream, at room temperature (do not use a "light"
*   substitute; it won't have enough body)*
1/2 cup heavy cream, at room temperature
1/4 cup (1 juicy lemon) fresh lemon juice
1/4 teaspoon mace or nutmeg
1/8 teaspoon salt
Finely shredded zest of 2 lemons

This cheesecake needs 12 to 24 hours to mellow before decorating. TO
MAKE THE FILLING, heat the oven to 400°F. Set the springform pan with
the prepared crust on a rimmed baking sheet (a little butter always seems

to seep from the crust). Brush the sides of the pan with butter. In a large mixing bowl, whisk the cream cheese until smooth and soft (beating with a mixer forces in more air than the custard can use, resulting in a coarse texture, thus the whisk). Whisking until smooth and well blended after each addition, add the sugar, then the eggs, one at a time, then the sour cream, heavy cream, lemon juice, mace, and salt. If the mixture has any lumps, pass it through a sieve. Stir in the zest. Pour the custard over the crust into the pan.

BAKE IN THE MIDDLE OF THE OVEN. After 15 minutes, turn the temperature down to 225°F. Bake 2 1/2 hours longer. At this point, a toothpick will emerge with a coating, indicating the cake's not done, but it will continue cooking out of the oven. This baking temperature and time makes a particularly creamy cheesecake. If it cracks upon cooling, don't worry—the pears will cover the crack. Set the cake on a rack at room temperature out of a draft to cool completely, then cover and refrigerate 12 to 24 hours before proceeding.

Burgundy-Poached Pears and their Glaze

2 cups sipping-quality burgundy or other dry red wine
2 cups cool water
1/2 cup granulated sugar
The peel of 1 lemon, removed with a vegetable peeler
1 or 2 cinnamon sticks
2 large (1 pound) firm ripe pears, peeled, cored, and sliced
   1/4-inch thick
1 tablespoon brandy, kirsch, or maraschino liqueur (optional)

TO POACH THE PEARS, in a large nonreactive skillet, cook the wine, water, sugar, peel, and cinnamon sticks over high heat until the sugar dissolves, stirring occasionally. Add the pears, bring to a simmer, reduce the heat, and simmer until the slices are deep burgundy in color, tender, and almost translucent, about 15 minutes. Turn into a bowl and cool, pushing the slices under the syrup occasionally. When cool, lift the slices onto toweling to drain, then wrap airtight.

To make the glaze, turn the syrup into a nonreactive skillet and boil over highest heat until reduced to about 1/3 cup. Blend with the spirits, if used, and reserve this glaze. MAKE-AHEAD NOTE: The slices can keep in their syrup several days, covered and refrigerated, before proceeding with the glaze. The glaze and the wrapped pear slices can wait a couple of hours.

To assemble the cheesecake, up to 8 hours before serving, remove the cake from the pan (release the spring, slide a spatula beneath the crust to free it from the bottom, then lift the cake with two pancake turners) and slide it onto a platter. Starting at the outside edge of the cake, closely overlap pear slices in circles over the top. In the center, finish with one slice tightly curled to resemble a flower bud. Warm the glaze, if necessary, and spoon or brush it over the pears to make them glisten. Refrigerate until an hour before serving, then remove to room temperature. Arrange the candles (ivory- or wine-colored) by lifting a pear slice and slipping the candle beside it into the cake. Plant a banner of greeting to one side, to preserve the center of the sunburst.

An ice would be too much.

Our birthday, of course,
is the anniversary of our birth upon this earth.
The word anniversary
is from the Latin annus, "year,"
and versus, "turned/turning."
An anniversary, then,
is one revolution of the sun later,
a returning of the earth
to that place where the heavenly bodies were
on the day of our birth.

American Traditions

THE BE-ALL AND END-ALL OF
BIG RICH OLD-FASHIONED MILK CHOCOLATE CAKE
WITH HERSHEY BAR CHOCOLATE FROSTING

*Three tall light layers of sink-into-me chocolate butter cake
filled and frosted with the glorious milk chocolate
of your—or your mother's—youth.*

TIPSY KENTUCKY BOURBON PECAN CAKE
WITH PEACH SAUCE

*Fine pound cake studded with pecans, drenched in Good Company,
and sauced with peaches.*

COUNTRY BLACKBERRY JAM CAKE

*Two light buttermilk cake layers perfumed with blackberries and spices,
thick with pecans and muscat raisins,
filled and topped with blackberry jam and blackberries,
and finished with pecan-strewn whipped cream.*

GREAT WHITE ALMOND CAKE
AFTER MARY TODD LINCOLN'S

Elegant almond-sprinkled almond cake with almond paste icing.

Rich Old-Fashioned

The Be-All and End-All of a

Milk Chocolate Cake with Hershey's

HAPPY BIRTHDAY!

bar chocolate frosting

HERSHEY'S

The Be-All and End-All of Big Rich Old Fashioned Milk Chocolate Cake with Hershey Bar Chocolate Frosting

Three tall light layers of sink-into-me chocolate butter cake filled and frosted with the glorious milk chocolate of your—or your mother's—youth.

To help me through the humiliation of a "D" in seventh grade gym class... the sadness of my best friend's moving a thousand miles away... the pain of not being asked to The Big Dance...my father brought home an incredibly tall and luscious chocolate cake in a bright pink box. Comfort food before it was known as comfort food. Then for a birthday when comfort is called for, make the cake that wraps the child within a mantle of pure chocolate love.

MAKES 16 SERVINGS

FOR THE PANS: *a firm lump of unsalted butter*
3 1/2 cups sifted cake flour
1/2 tablespoon baking soda
1/2 teaspoon baking powder
1/2 tablespoon salt
6 ounces unsweetened chocolate
1 cup water
16 tablespoons (2 sticks) unsalted butter, softened to the consistency of mayonnaise
2 cups granulated sugar
1/2 cup (firmly packed) light brown sugar, lumps crushed
1 1/2 tablespoons pure vanilla extract
6 extra-large eggs, warmed in their shells
1 cup buttermilk or soured milk, at room temperature (see NOTE)
Hershey Bar Chocolate Frosting (recipe follows)
Chocolate Piping, page 17 (optional)

NOTE: *To sour milk, place 1 tablespoon fresh lemon juice or mild vinegar at the bottom of the measure and fill to 1 cup with sweet milk. Set in a warm place a few minutes to clabber.*

TO MAKE THE CAKE, heat the oven to 350°F. Run the lump of butter over the bottoms of three 9-by-1 1/2-inch round cake pans, smooth a round of waxed paper into each, then butter the papers. Sift the flour, baking soda, baking powder, and salt together. In a medium heatproof bowl over (not in) barely simmering water, melt the chocolate in the 1 cup water, stirring occasionally until perfectly smooth. Remove from the heat. In a large mixing bowl, beat the butter on medium speed until creamy. Continue beating while sprinkling in both sugars a tablespoon at a time. Add the vanilla and beat until very light. Add the eggs one at a time, beating until thoroughly blended after each, then beat until very light and creamy. Blend in the chocolate. Add the flour in three parts (sprinkling it over the bowl), alternating with the buttermilk in two parts —beat on the lowest speed manageable and just until each addition disappears. Now fold the batter with a large flexible rubber spatula to finish blending thoroughly. Divide the batter among the pans, smoothing the tops, then pushing the batter slightly up against the sides. Bake 2 layers on the middle rack and 1 on the lower rack—stagger them so the top layers are not directly above the bottom one. Bake until a toothpick emerges clean from the center of the cakes, 30 to 35 minutes. Cool in the pans on racks 15 minutes, then turn out onto the racks, top sides up, to cool completely. MAKE-AHEAD NOTE: Present this glory the day of baking.

Hershey Bar Frosting

MAKES A SCANT 4 CUPS

5 cups confectioners' sugar, sifted if at all lumpy
3/4 cup unsweetened (not Dutch process) cocoa
7 tablespoons whole milk
14 tablespoons (1 3/4 sticks) unsalted butter, softened
14 ounces (2 giant bars) Hershey's milk chocolate, melted
2 tablespoons pure vanilla extract

To make the frosting, in a food processor or mixing bowl, blend the sugar and cocoa. Melt the butter with the milk at half-power in the microwave or over low heat. Add while hot to the sugar with the chocolate and vanilla. Process or beat until smooth. If too thick, add a thread more hot milk; if too thin, add more sugar. Spread at once. Make-ahead note: This fudgy frosting, so quickly made, loses quality if resoftened after setting.

To assemble the cake, up to 6 hours before serving, set the thickest layer on a platter, bottom side up. Spread with 2/3 cup of the frosting. Set on the second layer, also bottoms-up, frost it, then set on the top layer, top side up. Frost the top and sides of the cake, making big sweeps of curls in the frosting with your knife, in a regular pattern or willy nilly—but if you plan to pipe a greeting, make it smooth across the center of the top. This is one majestic cake that wants and needs no further decoration. When the frosting has set, pipe a message in dark chocolate, if you choose to. Keep on the cool side of room temperature until serving. Just before serving, plant a banner of greeting (if you're using one) and arrange the candles.

For an ice, it's got to be pure vanilla ice cream.

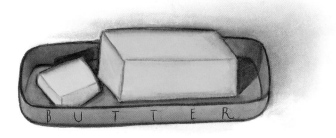

Th' past always looks better than it was.
It's only pleasant because it isn't here.
—Finley Peter Dunne
A Family Reunion

Tipsy Kentucky Bourbon Pecan Cake with Peach Sauce

Fine pound cake studded with pecans,
drenched in Good Company, and sauced with peaches.

Dolley Madison discreetly flavored her pound cake—one pound each of
butter, sugar, flour, and eggs—with brandy and rosewater.
A century later, my grandmother, with a fondness for baking and bourbon,
sloshed Dixie nectar into her pound cake instead.
And where there was sour mash, there were sweet pecans—
best throw them in, too. My grandmother served the cake at her card parties
to celebrate a friend's birthday, or whatever occasion came to mind.

MAKES 14 SERVINGS

FOR THE PAN: *2 to 3 tablespoons of soft unsalted butter and 2 to*
3 tablespoons of all-purpose flour
2 1/4 cups sifted cake flour

1 tablespoon plus 1/8 teaspoon baking powder
1/2 teaspoon salt
16 tablespoons (2 sticks) unsalted butter, softened to the
  consistency of mayonnaise
1 1/2 cups plus 1/2 cup granulated sugar
5 extra-large eggs, warmed in their shells
3 fluid ounces plus 1 cup (or to taste) sipping-quality bourbon
2 cups (7 ounces) toasted pecan halves
Peach Sauce *(recipe follows)*
Long branches of fresh unsprayed mint, for the decoration

TO MAKE THE CAKE, a day or two before planning to serve, heat the oven to 350°F. Brush both bottom and sides of one 8 1/4-by-3 1/4 to 9 1/2-by-3 1/2-inch tube or bundt pan with butter. Coat with flour, then knock out the excess. Sift the flour, baking powder, and salt together. In a large mixing bowl, beat the butter on medium speed until creamy. Continue beating while sprinkling in 1 1/2 cups of the sugar a tablespoon at a time, then beat until very light. Add the eggs, one at a time, beating until blended after each, then beat until very light and creamy. Add the flour in three parts (sprinkling it over the bowl), alternating with 3 ounces bourbon in two parts—beat on the lowest speed manageable and just until each addition disappears. Sprinkle over the pecans and fold the batter with a large flexible rubber spatula to finish blending thoroughly. Smooth into the pan, slightly pushing the batter up against the sides and the tube.

BAKE IN THE MIDDLE OF THE OVEN until a toothpick comes out clean from the center of the cake, 55 to 60 minutes. Heat 1/2 cup of the remaining bourbon and 1/4 cup of the remaining sugar together, stirring until the sugar dissolves. Pierce the top all over with a fork, then pour the syrup evenly over the cake. Cool 15 minutes in the pan on a rack, then turn out onto the rack, rumpled side up, to cool completely. When cool, heat the rest of the bourbon and sugar as before. Set the cake smooth side up, pierce as before, and pour over the syrup. MAKE-AHEAD NOTE: If possible, the cake should mellow a day in a cool place before serving. Wrap airtight. The cake will keep fresh a couple of days.

Peach Sauce

1/4 cup fresh orange juice
1 tablespoon fresh lemon juice
1 1/3 cups best-quality peach preserves or jam (if unavailable,
use apricot preserves), warmed
4 cups peeled and coarsely chopped fresh peaches (6 to 8) or
thawed drained premium-quality frozen peach slices

TO MAKE THE SAUCE, in a food processor or mixing bowl, blend the orange and lemon juices, then add the preserves and briefly blend. Turn into a bowl, add the peaches and stir gently until each slice has been moistened. Chill, tightly covered, at least 1 hour. MAKE-AHEAD NOTE: The sauce will be at its best for about 4 hours.

TO ASSEMBLE THE CAKE, just before serving, unwrap the cake and set it, smooth side up, on a platter. Plant a banner of greeting and arrange the (peach-colored) candles, tucking a mint leaf or two beside each candle. Garland the bottom with branches of mint. Serve each piece of cake on a plate, encircled with Peach Sauce.

FOR AN ICE, a complement of peaches, page 115.

Symbolism of Birthday Gems and Flowers

JANUARY:
garnet—truth and constancy
carnation—admiration

FEBRUARY:
amethyst—sincerity
violet—modesty and simplicity

MARCH:
bloodstone—courage
daffodil—regard

APRIL:
diamond—innocence and light
daisy—gentleness and innocence

MAY:
emerald—success in love
lily-of-the-valley—purity and humility

JUNE:
pearl—purity
rose—love and desire

JULY:
ruby—courage
water lily—eloquence and persuasion

AUGUST:
sardonyx—ensures marital happiness
poppy—imagination and dreaminess

SEPTEMBER:
sapphire—magical properties
aster—elegance and daintiness

OCTOBER:
opal—hope
calendula—obedience

NOVEMBER:
topaz—fidelity
chrysanthemum—cheerfulness and optimism

DECEMBER:
turquoise—prosperity
holly—foresight and defense

Country Blackberry Jam Cake

*Two light buttermilk cake layers perfumed with blackberries
and spices, thick with pecans and muscat raisins,
filled and topped with blackberry jam and blackberries,
and finished with pecan-strewn whipped cream.*

In berry season, I must get out to the orchard early to beat the birds
to our share of blackberries, blackcap raspberries, and tayberries.
The bluejays are brazen, but if I move fast enough,
I'll have ample berries for jam and for strewing over this beautiful cake
for our granddaughter's August birthday.
Too little made, this cake is a jewel.

MAKES 12 SERVINGS

FOR THE PANS: *a firm lump of unsalted butter*
1/2 cup seeded muscat or other large dark raisins
1/2 cup toasted pecans—halved or chopped (see NOTE*), plus*
2/3 cup toasted halves, for the decoration
2 tablespoons plus 2 cups sifted cake flour
1 teaspoon baking soda
1 teaspoon cinnamon
1 teaspoon nutmeg

1/2 teaspoon ground cloves

8 tablespoons (1 stick) unsalted butter, softened to the
consistency of mayonnaise

3/4 cup granulated sugar

4 extra-large eggs, warmed in their shells

1 cup thick seedless blackberry or black raspberry jam, plus 3/4
cup for the filling and top

1/4 cup buttermilk or soured milk, at room temperature (see NOTE*)*

1 1/2 cups fresh blackberries or other member of the family, for
the filling and the decoration

1 1/2 cups cold heavy cream, whipped

NOTE ON PECANS: *Pecan halves make a crunchy mouthful but the*
slice can crumble as you wrestle with the nut. Chopped nuts
make perfect slices.

NOTE: *To sour milk, place a scant teaspoon fresh lemon juice or*
mild vinegar at the bottom of the measure and fill to 1/4 cup with
sweet milk. Set in a warm place a few minutes to clabber.

TO MAKE THE CAKE, heat the oven to 350°F. Run the lump of butter over
the bottoms of two 9-by-1 1/2-inch round cake pans, smooth a round of
waxed paper into each, then butter the papers. In a bowl, toss the raisins
and 1/2 cup of the pecans with the 2 tablespoons flour separating the
raisins it stuck together. Sift the 2 cups flour, soda, cinnamon, nutmeg,
and cloves together. In a large mixing bowl, beat the butter on medium
speed until creamy. Continue beating while sprinkling in the sugar a
tablespoon at a time, then beat until very light. Add the eggs, one at a
time, beating until blended after each, then beat until very light and
creamy. Add the flour in three parts (sprinkling it over the bowl), alternating with 1 cup of the jam and the buttermilk in two parts—beat on
the lowest speed manageable and just until each addition disappears.
Sprinkle over the raisin-pecan mixture and fold the batter with a large
flexible rubber spatula to finish blending thoroughly. Divide the batter
between the pans, smoothing the tops, and slightly pushing the batter
up against the sides.

BAKE BOTH PANS IN THE MIDDLE OF THE OVEN, staggering them on the rack. Bake until a toothpick emerges clean from the center of the cakes, about 30 minutes. Cool in the pans on the racks 15 minutes, then turn out onto the racks, top sides up, to cool completely. MAKE-AHEAD NOTE: Serve this cake the day of baking.

TO ASSEMBLE THE CAKE, up to 2 hours before serving, set the thickest layer, bottom side up, on a platter. Spread with a rounded 1/3 cup of the remaining jam. Sprinkle with 3/4 cup of the berries. Set the second layer over the first, top side up, and repeat. Frost the sides with the whipped cream. Sprinkle the remaining 2/3 cup pecan halves over the whipped cream. Keep on the cool side of room temperature until serving. Just before serving, plant a banner of greeting and arrange the (berry-colored) candles.

FOR AN ICE, the lively contrast of orange, page 116.

Time was
on the day of a baby's birth
in England,
the child was given water into which a red-hot ember—
glowing symbol of life—
had been dropped.
In Ireland,
a boy received honey
on the tip of his father's sword
to make him a warrior.
And in Scotland,
sap from a green ash tree
was mixed with honey
to protect him from fairies.

Great White Almond Cake after Mary Todd Lincoln's

Elegant almond-sprinkled almond cake with almond paste icing.

Created in 1825 for Lafayette's visit to Lexington, the receipt
for this splendid cake was given to Kentucky Senator Robert Todd's family.
Years later, "plump, swift, beaming" Mary Todd (the description is
Carl Sandburg's) baked the cake for her husband, Abe Lincoln,
who thought it "the best I ever ate."
Mace and brandy and almond icing enhance it further. A man's cake.

MAKES 16 SERVINGS

FOR THE MOLD: *2 1/2 tablespoons soft unsalted butter; 1 cup
(about 3 1/2 ounces) toasted sliced almonds, plus 1 cup for the
decoration, and about 2 tablespoons granulated sugar*
3 cups sifted cake flour
4 teaspoons baking powder
1 teaspoon ground mace
*16 tablespoons (2 sticks) unsalted butter, softened to the
consistency of mayonnaise*
2 cups granulated sugar
1/4 cup sipping-quality brandy
1 cup (3 2/3 ounces) finely ground blanched almonds (see NOTE*)*
1 cup whole milk, at room temperature
*1 cup (7 extra-large) egg whites, warmed in their shells before
separating*
1/2 teaspoon salt
Almond Paste Icing *(recipe follows)*

Unsprayed flowers in soft colors: a slender branch of apple blossoms or hollyhocks (remove blossoms on one side so the branch will lie flat), or a sheaf of lavender or dried edible grains, for the decoration
Chocolate Piping, *page 17 (optional)*
NOTE: *Add 1 tablespoon of the flour to the almonds when grinding to keep them from becoming oily.*

TO MAKE THE CAKE, heat the oven to 350°F. Prepare the mold by generously buttering one 9 1/2-by-3 1/2-inch bundt pan. Coat the inside with 3/4 cup of the sliced almonds, then sprinkle with about 2 tablespoons sugar to fill the interspaces. Sift the flour, baking powder, and mace together. In a large mixing bowl, beat the butter on medium speed until creamy. Continue beating while sprinkling in 1 1/3 cups of the sugar, a tablespoon at a time, then beat until very light. Blend in the brandy, then the ground almonds. Add the flour in three parts (sprinkling it over the bowl), alternating with the milk in two parts—beat on the lowest speed manageable and just until each addition has disappeared. Set aside. With clean beaters, beat the whites in a large mixing bowl on low speed until frothy. Add the salt and beat on medium speed until soft peaks form. Beat on high speed while sprinkling in the remaining 2/3 cup sugar, a tablespoon at a time. Beat just until the peak in the bowl holds, then flops, when you lift the beaters. Add one third of the whites to the batter and blend in with a flat wire whisk or the mixer on low speed. Add the remaining whites and fold the batter with a large flexible rubber spatula to finish blending thoroughly. Smooth into the pan, slightly pushing the batter up against the sides. Sprinkle with 1/4 cup sliced almonds remaining from the mold and a little sugar.

BAKE IN THE MIDDLE OF THE OVEN until a broomstraw or thin metal skewer comes out clean from the center of the cake, 55 to 60 minutes. Cool in the pan on a rack 15 minutes, then turn out onto the rack, bottom side up, to cool completely. MAKE-AHEAD NOTE: Unfrosted and wrapped airtight, the cake will keep fresh in a cool place up to 5 days.

Almond Paste Icing

7 to 8 ounces almond paste, softened
3 cups confectioners' sugar sifted if at all lumpy
1 tablespoon rose water or pure vanilla extract
5 to 7 tablespoons whole milk or cream

TO MAKE THE ICING, in a food processor or with a mixer at medium speed, blend the almond paste with the sugar and flavoring. Slowly add milk until the frosting is of spreading consistency (be careful not to over-process or it will thin out). MAKE-AHEAD NOTE: This may be tightly covered and refrigerated up to 4 days. Bring to room temperature before applying.

TO ASSEMBLE THE CAKE, up to 6 hours before serving, set the cake on a platter. Spoon the icing over the top and let it slip down the sides, allowing some of the almond-spangled cake to show. Leaving space for a greeting (should you choose to pipe one), while the icing is moist, sprinkle the remaining 1 cup of sliced almonds over it. Keep on the cool side of room temperature until serving. Just before serving, lay the branch or stalks of flowers across the top of the cake to one side. Pipe a message or plant a banner of greeting and arrange the (ivory-colored) candles.

FOR AN ICE, sprightly cranberry, page 115.

Traditionally in China and other parts of the East,
only important people celebrated their birthday—
everyone else simply became one year older
on the New Year.
With the early Greeks,
only the birthdays of the gods were important,
but they had birthdays every month—
Athena, Ares, and Saturn on the third...
Aphrodite, Hermes, and Heracles on the fourth...
Artemis on the sixth...
Apollo on the seventh, and so on.

Milestones

SWEET SIXTEEN
CHOCOLATE-PEPPERMINT CANDY CAKE

*Two chocolate-peppermint buttermilk cake layers filled and frosted
with billowy white peppermint frosting and
rosy with crushed peppermint candy.*

A COMING-OF-AGE *ZUPPA INGLESE*

*Four layers of orange-almond butter sponge cake sprinkled with
marsala and rum, filled with orange, vanilla, and almond custards,
and slathered with whipped cream—
the heavenly Italian way with English trifle.*

A DAZZLING VENETIAN SWEET
FOR A DIAMOND BIRTHDAY

Strangolapreti—*Priest Strangler*—*is an exotic confection of fruits and
nuts bound with rum syrup-moistened morsels of exquisite sponge cake,
wrapped in rosettes of whipped cream, and strewn with rose petals.*

Sweet Sixteen
Chocolate-Peppermint Candy Cake

*Two chocolate-peppermint buttermilk cake layers
filled and frosted with billowy white peppermint frosting
and rosy with crushed peppermint candy.*

For my sixteenth birthday, my mother surprised me
with a small luncheon at the Beverly Hills Hotel. Pink was
the hotel's signature color, and dessert was a peppermint candy cake.
These days, sixteen-year-olds are worlds more sophisticated,
but it occurs to me that peppermint has both sweetness and snap.

MAKES 12 SERVINGS

FOR THE PAN: *a firm lump of unsalted butter*
2 1/2 cups sifted cake flour
1 1/4 teaspoons baking soda
1/2 teaspoon salt
16 tablespoons (2 sticks) unsalted butter, softened to the
  consistency of mayonnaise

1 cup granulated sugar
3/4 cup (firmly packed) light brown sugar, lumps crushed
1/2 tablespoon pure peppermint extract
4 extra-large eggs, warmed in their shells
4 ounces unsweetened chocolate, melted
1 1/2 cups buttermilk or soured milk, at room temperature (see NOTE*)*
Billowy White Peppermint Frosting *(recipe follows)*
About 12 ounces pink peppermint candy, coarsely crushed, for
    the decoration
Chocolate Piping, *page 17 (optional)*
Unsprayed pink blossoms such as pinks, baby roses, tulips, or
    tuberous begonias, for the decoration
NOTE: *To sour milk, place 1 1/2 tablespoons fresh lemon juice or*
mild vinegar at the bottom of the measure and fill to 1 1/2 cups
with sweet milk. Set in a warm place a few minutes to clabber.

TO MAKE THE CAKE, heat the oven to 350°F. Run the lump of butter over
the bottoms of two 9-by-1 1/2-inch round cake pans, smooth a round of
waxed paper into each, and butter the papers. Sift the flour, baking soda,
and salt together. In a large mixing bowl, beat the butter on medium speed
until creamy. Continue beating while sprinkling in the granulated and
brown sugars, a tablespoon at a time. Add the peppermint extract and beat
until very light. Add the eggs, one at a time, beating until blended after
each, then beat until very light and creamy. Blend in the chocolate. Blend
in the flour in three parts (sprinkling it over the bowl), alternating with the
buttermilk in two parts—beat on the lowest manageable speed and just until
each addition disappears. Divide the batter between the pans, smoothing
the tops, and slightly pushing the batter up against the sides.

BAKE BOTH PANS IN THE MIDDLE OF THE OVEN, staggering them on the
rack. Bake until a toothpick emerges clean from the center of the cakes,
about 35 minutes. Cool on racks in the pans 15 minutes, then turn out
onto racks, top sides up, to cool completely. MAKE-AHEAD NOTE: The
unfrosted layers are lightest the day of baking, but wrapped airtight,
they'll keep fresh in a cool place a day or two.

Billowy White Peppermint Frosting

MAKES ABOUT 4 CUPS

3/4 cup granulated sugar
1/4 cup white corn syrup
2 tablespoons water
2 extra-large egg whites
1/4 teaspoon cream of tartar
1/4 teaspoon salt
1 teaspoon pure peppermint extract

TO MAKE THE FROSTING, in a 2-quart top of a double boiler or heatproof bowl, use a portable mixer on low speed or rotary beater to blend the sugar, corn syrup, water, egg whites, cream of tartar, and salt. Set over (not in) simmering water on medium heat. Beat at high speed just until the frosting holds a peak when you lift the beaters, 4 to 5 minutes with the mixer, 7 minutes by hand. *Do not overcook.* Remove from the heat, add the peppermint extract, and beat at high speed until the frosting is cool and divinely billowy, another minute or two or three. Use at once.

TO ASSEMBLE THE CAKE, up to 6 hours before serving, set the thickest layer, bottom side up, on a platter. Smooth over 2/3 cup of the frosting, then set on the second layer, top side up. Frost the top and sides of the cake. If you plan to pipe a greeting, outline it at once. While the frosting is moist, sprinkle the candy generously over the sides and on top, leaving room for the piping or covering the entire top. Pipe the message, if you choose to. Keep on the cool side of room temperature until serving. Just before serving, plant a banner of greeting (if you're using one). Lay a single flower on top of the cake. Arrange the (deep pink) candles and garland the rim of the cake plate with the remaining flowers.

FOR AN ICE, fresh peppermint, page 117.

Traditionally, in Mexico
it is the fifteenth birthday—
the age at which she may begin receiving suitors—
that is significant for a girl.
A gala party is given in her honor at night,
with colored lanterns
and mariachis—*strolling musicians.*

A Coming of Age Zuppa Inglese

*Four layers of orange-almond butter sponge cake sprinkled with
marsala and rum, filled with orange, vanilla, and almond custards,
and slathered with whipped cream—
the heavenly Italian way with English trifle.*

When our eldest turned twenty-one, we threw a party
and I made *Zuppa Inglese* for his cake.   He'd loved this "English Soup"
when I'd made it for the eightieth birthday
of my father's old friend, Groucho Marx, who had also adored it.
Spirited, luscious, and memorable at any age,
the dessert is based on the invaluable French butter sponge cake, *génoise.*

MAKES 12 SERVINGS

FOR THE PANS: *a firm lump of unsalted butter*
1 cup less 2 tablespoons sifted all-purpose flour
1/2 cup less 1 tablespoon sifted cake flour
1 teaspoon pure almond extract
Grated zest of 2 oranges
8 tablespoons (1 stick) unsalted butter, melted
2 cups (8 extra-large) eggs, warmed in their shells before
measuring
1 cup granulated sugar, plus 1 tablespoon, for the whipped cream
Orange, Vanilla, and Almond Custards *(recipe follows)*
2/3 cup light marsala
1/2 cup light rum
2 cups cold heavy cream
A small bouquet of unsprayed rustic flowers such as red marigolds,
geraniums, or nasturtiums; yellow sunflowers, mustard blossoms,
or daylilies; and blue-to-purple borage blossoms, sage blossoms,
or lilacs, for the decoration
A length of thin red fabric ribbon to tie a small bouquet, for the
decoration

TO MAKE THE CAKE, heat the oven to 350°F. Run the lump of butter over the bottoms of two 9-by-1 1/2-inch round cake pans, smooth a round of waxed paper into each, then butter the papers. Sift the two flours together. Add the almond extract and orange zest to the butter. In a very large mixing bowl, beat the eggs and 1 cup of the sugar together at high speed. Beat until the beaters make tracks in the mixture and it has become so thick that, when you lift the beaters, the batter mounds up on the surface a second or two before sinking—6 to 7 minutes. Sprinkle over half the flour and, with a balloon whisk or large flexible rubber spatula, blend in thoroughly—10 to 15 big airy strokes. Sprinkle over the remaining flour, then fold while you drizzle in the butter-zest mixture, another 10 to 15 strokes. If you've used a whisk, now fold the batter with a large flexible rubber spatula to finish blending thoroughly, 8 or 9 strokes. Quickly divide the batter between the pans and set in the middle of the oven.

BAKE UNTIL GOLDEN BROWN and the tops spring back when lightly tapped, 22 to 25 minutes (don't open the door before 20 minutes, and then just a crack, or the cakes might fall). Immediately run a knife around the edges of the pans and turn out the layers onto racks, bottom side up, to cool completely. MAKE-AHEAD NOTE: Wrapped airtight, the layers keep fresh 2 to 3 days at room temperature.

Orange, Vanilla and Almond Custards

MAKES 4 1/3 CUPS CUSTARD

3/4 cup granulated sugar
1/3 cup plus 1 tablespoon cornstarch
Pinch of salt
4 cups whole milk
3 extra-large eggs
1 egg yolk
1 teaspoon pure orange extract
1/2 tablespoon pure vanilla extract
1/2 teaspoon pure almond extract

No matter how careful you are, if you cook the custard directly over the burner, the bottom will brown and there will be small brown flecks in the custard. TO MAKE THE CUSTARDS, in the top of a double boiler or saucepan that will nest in a bigger pot, blend the sugar, cornstarch, and salt. Whisk in some of the milk to make a smooth paste, then slowly whisk in the remaining milk. Whisk continually over lowest heat just until the milk is hot, then set over simmering water. Whisk until the mixture bubbles and thickens. Whisk the eggs and extra yolk in a medium bowl until blended, then whisk a stream of the hot mixture into the eggs until they thicken. Whisk this mixture back into the pot. Cook, stirring constantly with a wooden spoon, 5 minutes, then put the custard through a sieve. Divide the custard among three bowls—a scant 1 1/2 cups each. Blend the orange extract into one bowl, the vanilla into another, and the almond into the third. Lay waxed paper or plastic film directly on the surfaces of the custards to keep skins from forming, cover tightly and chill at least 4 hours. MAKE-AHEAD NOTE: The custards may be prepared and refrigerated a day in advance.

TO ASSEMBLE THE ZUPPA, from 4 to 12 hours before serving, split the two layers horizontally in half (page 15). You'll need a plate about 10 inches wide with a lip. Set the thickest layer, cut side up, on the plate. Blend the marsala and rum in a bowl. Fill a 1/4-cup measure with the blend and sprinkle it evenly over the first layer. Spread with the orange custard. Yes, I know it's soupy—that's the reason for the lip on the plate—but try to get it all to stay on the cake. Set a second layer, cut side up, on the custard, sprinkle over another 1/4 cup spirits, and cover with the vanilla custard. Repeat with the third layer, more spirits, and the almond custard. Top with the last layer, cut side down, and sprinkle with the remaining spirits. With plastic film, wrap the whole plate—this will hold the layers in place while the custard firms up—and chill from 4 to 12 hours. Whip the cream with the remaining 1 tablespoon sugar.

JUST BEFORE SERVING, use two pancake turners to lift the cake to a platter. Swirl the whipped cream over the top and sides of the cake. Tie a few flowers into a bouquet with the ribbon and lay on top, arrange the (red or blue or yellow) candles, plant a banner of greeting, and garland the platter with more flowers. Serve in wedges.

FOR AN ICE, *niente*—nothing. It would be gilding the lily.

In Italy, particularly from Rome south,
you receive presents and a cake
not on the anniversary of your birth,
but on your saint's day—
the day of the saint after whom you were named,
the saint who protects you.
If your saint also happens to be the patron of your town,
then there are cakes and processions aplenty.

A Dazzling Venetian Sweet for a Diamond Birthday

Strangolapreti—*Priest Strangler*—*is an exotic confection of fruits and nuts bound with rum syrup-moistened morsels of exquisite sponge cake, wrapped in rosettes of whipped cream, and strewn with rose petals.*

But what priest thus swallowed his fate?
From Venice, crossroads of the trading world, come almonds
introduced by ancient Greeks, walnuts from Roman-planted groves,
raisins dried by Greco-Roman methods, kernels of stone pines
once sacred to Neptune, sweet oranges and lemons from Arabian caravans,
cinnamon from Ceylon, cane sugar from India, chocolate from Central America
and rum from Hispaniola. All bound together with ephemeral wisps of cake.
Smashing for one who has Seen-and-Eaten-It-All, and fun for you to make.

MAKES 16 SERVINGS

For the Sponge Cake

FOR THE PAN: *a firm lump of unsalted butter*
3/4 cup sifted cake flour
1/4 cup plus 2 tablespoons sifted cornstarch
1/2 teaspoon plus 1/8 teaspoon baking powder
1/4 teaspoon salt
1 cup (7 extra-large) egg whites, warmed in their shells before
* separating*
1/2 cup (6 extra-large) egg yolks, warmed in their shells before
* separating*
Scant 1/3 cup lukewarm water
2 tablespoons fresh lemon juice
1/2 tablespoon pure vanilla extract
3/4 cup plus 2 tablespoons granulated sugar
1/2 teaspoon cream of tartar

TO MAKE THE CAKE, heat the oven to 350°F. Run the lump of butter over the bottom of one 10-inch tube pan, smooth in a ring of waxed paper to line the bottom, then butter the paper. Sift the flour, cornstarch, baking powder, and salt together. Turn the separated eggs into 2 large mixing bowls. Beat the yolks at high speed until fluffy and creamy. Continue beating while you slowly drizzle in the water, lemon juice, and vanilla extract. Beat until frothy and increased in volume, then continue beating while sprinkling in 3/4 cup of the sugar, a tablespoon at a time. Beat until, when you lift the beaters, the batter mounds up on the surface a second or two before sinking. Set aside. Immediately, with clean beaters, beat the whites at low speed until frothy. Add the cream of tartar and beat on medium speed until soft peaks form. Beat on high speed while sprinkling in the remaining 2 tablespoons sugar, a tablespoon at a time. Continue beating just until the peak in the bowl holds, then flops when you lift the beaters. Add one third of the whites to the yolk mixture and blend in with a flat wire whisk or large flexible rubber spatula. Sprinkle the flour mixture evenly over the yolk mixture and fold until *almost* completely blended in. Add the remaining whites and fold the batter with a large flexible rubber spatula to finish blending thoroughly. Smooth into the pan, slightly pushing the batter up against the tube and the sides.

BAKE IN THE MIDDLE OF THE OVEN until a toothpick emerges clean from the center of the cake, 35 to 45 minutes. Immediately invert the pan and either stand it on its feet or hang from the neck of a bottle until the cake is cold. MAKE-AHEAD NOTE: Wrapped airtight and kept in a cool place, the cake will keep fresh up to 5 days.

For the Strangolapreti

FOR THE PAN: *a firm lump of unsalted butter*
1/2 cup plus 2 tablespoons white rum
1 cup golden raisins
2 cups broken toasted walnuts
1 cup toasted pine nuts (see Note)
1 cup finely chopped toasted almonds
1 1/4 cups granulated sugar
1/2 cup cool water
Finely shredded zest of 2 oranges
2 teaspoons unsweetened cocoa (either sort)
Rounded 1/4 teaspoon cinnamon
*The sponge cake (if you're pressed for time and need to purchase
    one, it should weigh 16 ounces)*
1/4 cup finely diced candied lemon peel
2 cups cold heavy cream, whipped
*"Silver" leaves (from a party store or Maid of Scandinavia, page
    17), for the decoration*
A handful of unsprayed rose petals, any color, for the decoration
NOTE: *If you don't want the flavor of pine nuts to be slightly
dominant, use 1/4 cup less pine nuts and 1/4 cup more walnuts.*

TO MAKE THE STRANGOLAPRETI—do this the day before serving—bring 1/2 cup of the rum to a simmer, pour it over the raisins in a small bowl, then cover and set aside. Heat the oven to 375°F. Run the lump of butter over the bottom and sides of one 9-inch round cake pan with a volume of 7 cups (equivalent pans are on page 12). Smooth in a round of waxed paper to line the bottom, then butter the paper. Mix the walnuts, pine nuts, and almonds together.

To make the rum syrup, blend the sugar and water in a small saucepan over high heat, stirring until the syrup simmers. Add the orange zest, cover, remove from the heat, cool a bit, then whisk in the 2 tablespoons rum, the cocoa, and the cinnamon. Set aside. In a food processor or blender, process the sponge cake, a few hunks at a time, until reduced to pieces the size of seed pearls. Turn the morsels into a big bowl with the raisins and their rum, the nuts, and the candied peel. Pour over the rum syrup and toss lightly with a fork until the mixture is thoroughly blended. Smooth the mixture into the pan, evening the top (sometimes you must press it a bit to make everything fit).

Bake in the middle of the oven until toasty brown on top, about 40 minutes. Cool completely in the pan on a rack, then cover and refrigerate in the pan from 12 to 24 hours.

To make the decoration, in advance you might cut a "7" and a "5" from heavy cardboard, 3 1/2 to 4 inches tall. Wrap them smoothly in foil, shiny sides out, and white-glue thin bamboo skewers to the bottom so the numbers can stand in the cake. Cover both sides of the numbers completely with large faceted uncolored brilliants (choose them with catching the light in mind) from the crafts or dime store, fixing them with white glue.

To assemble the STRANGOLAPRETI, up to 2 hours before serving, free the sides of the cake with a thin knife, lay a platter upside down on top, and invert the cake onto it. If you are so inclined, pipe the whipped cream through a large rosette tube, covering the cake with creamy stars. If not, swirl on the cream thickly. Refrigerate until serving. Just before serving, plant the "7" and "5" or a banner of greeting in the center, arrange silver leaves around the border of the plate, strew the *strangolapreti* with rose petals, and arrange the (petal-colored) candles. Serve in wedges.

An ice would be too rich.

NINON DE LENCLOS,[1] ON HER LAST BIRTHDAY

So let me have the rouge again,
    And comb my hair the curly way.
The poor young men, the dear young men—
    They'll all be here by noon today.

And I shall wear the blue, I think—
    They beg to touch its rippled lace;
Or do they love me best in pink,
    So sweetly flattering the face?

And are you sure my eyes are bright,
    And is it true my cheek is clear?
Young what's-his-name stayed half the night;
    He vows to cut his throat, poor dear!

So bring my scarlet slippers, then,
    And fetch the powder-puff to me.
The dear young men, the poor young men—
    They think I'm only seventy!
                  —DOROTHY PARKER

1616-1706, Frenchwoman celebrated for her beauty, wit, and *amours*.

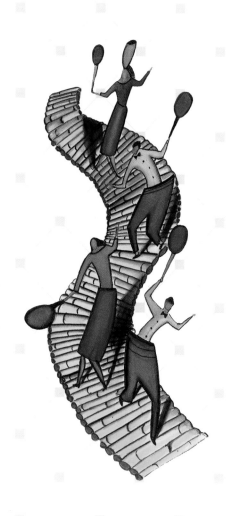

For Special Occasions

A FRESH BERRY-FILLED MERINGUE HEART
FOR THE NO-FAT NO-SALT NO-CHOLESTEROL
NO-WHEAT NO-NUTS NO-WORRY BIRTHDAY!

A gorgeous meringue heart overflowing with three colors of berries,
accompanied by blackberry water ice,
all topped with brilliant strawberry sauce.

LEMON CHIFFON CAKE
WITH PALE HONEY GLAZE AND LEAVES OF THYME
FOR A SICKABED BIRTHDAY

A light light light chiffon cake flavored and finished with
the sweet outdoors.

FRESH GINGER GINGERCAKE
FROSTED WITH GLOSSY CHOCOLATE
AND STUDDED WITH CHOCOLATE-DIPPED FRUIT
FOR A CROWD

One sumptuous layer of the old-fashioned favorite,
intensely flavored and frosted and luxuriously finished.

Heart for the No-fat

No-salt no-cholesterol no-wheat

Fresh Berry – filled Meringue

No-nuts no-worry Birthday!

A Fresh Berry-Filled Meringue Heart for the No-Fat No-Salt No-Cholesterol No-Wheat No-Nuts No-Worry Birthday!

A gorgeous meringue heart overflowing with three colors of berries, accompanied by blackberry water ice, all topped with brilliant strawberry sauce.

Matters of diet are so boring, both in the doing and the listening to. What pleasure to serve a birthday treat everyone can simply spoon up and enjoy!

10 SERVINGS

4 extra-large egg whites, warmed in their shells before separating
1/2 teaspoon cream of tartar
3/4 cup granulated sugar
1 teaspoon pure vanilla extract
1 cup sifted confectioners' sugar
Strawberry Sauce *(recipe follows)*
About 5 cups mixed fresh raspberries, blackberries, and
blueberries; if berries are unavailable, make a mix of the
prettiest fresh fruits the market affords—in winter, mix slices of
kiwi, chunks of pineapple, dark seedless grapes, and such
Blackberry Water Ice, *page 115*
A few handfuls of unsprayed strawberry, grape, or nasturtium
leaves, and a few lengths of their vines, for the decoration

TO MAKE THE PATTERN FOR THE HEART, draw and cut out a paper heart that pleases you, making it 9 to 10 inches at its widest and deepest points. (Fold the heart in half lengthwise to check symmetry, should you care about symmetry!)

Line a baking sheet with brown paper but do not butter it. In the center of the pan, outline the heart with pencil on the brown paper.

TO MAKE THE MERINGUE, heat the oven to 250°F. In a very large mixing bowl, beat the whites at low speed until frothy. Add the cream of tartar and beat on medium speed until soft peaks form. Beat on high speed while sprinkling in the granulated sugar, a tablespoon at a time—it's important that you take about 6 minutes to do this. Add the vanilla and beat another minute or two until the whites are very stiff and shiny. Sprinkle the sugar over the bowl all at once and blend on low speed just until it disappears. Now fold the meringue with a large flexible rubber spatula to finish blending thoroughly.

TO SHAPE THE HEART, use a spatula to smooth about half the meringue inside the lines. On top of the base around the edges, build the sides by piping the remaining meringue through a plain tube, or spooning it around the rim and shaping the sides with your finger or a spoon.

BAKE IN THE MIDDLE OF THE OVEN without opening the door for 1 1/2 hours— if the air is damp, bake 15 to 20 minutes more. Turn off the heat and don't open the oven for another 4 hours. Lift up the heart with a spatula, carefully peel off the paper, and set the heart on a rack at room temperature to finish cooling completely. MAKE-AHEAD NOTE: In a dry climate, kept in a cool dry peaceable place, the meringue may be baked at least a week in advance. In a damp climate, if stored in a tightly closed tin, it will also keep that long.

Strawberry Sauce

MAKES ABOUT 3 CUPS

4 1/2 cups fresh hulled sweet strawberries (out of season, berries
   frozen individually without sugar may be used—measure while
   frozen, because they collapse when thawed)
1 tablespoon fresh orange juice
About 1 1/2 tablespoons fresh lemon juice
2 1/2 or more tablespoons granulated sugar

To make the sauce, in a food processor or blender, purée the berries with the orange juice and 1 1/2 tablespoons lemon juice. Turn into a bowl and add sugar to taste, then perhaps a bit more lemon juice for point. Cover and chill. Make-ahead note: The sauce may be prepared several hours in advance, covered, and chilled. Bring to room temperature and stir well before serving.

To assemble the heart, at your convenience, use a toothpick to gently whittle holes around the rim for the (berry-colored) candles. Set the heart on a platter. Just before serving, heap the berries in the center, mixing the colors. Tuck leaves here and there in the berries, and set the rest of the leaves and the vines around the heart. Plant a banner of greeting (set on thin bamboo skewers) and set the candles around the rim. When you cut into it, expect the meringue to shatter. To serve, set a portion of meringue on the plate. Add a spoonful of the blackberry ice, cover meringue and ice with berries, then ladle a little lake of sauce around the edges.

Happy Birthday to You
*was written around the turn of the century
by Mildred J. and Patty S. Hill—
about the same time that birthday cards
appeared in the English-speaking world.
Birthday wishes are thought to be
magically effective
only when delivered early in the morning.*

Lemon Chiffon Cake with Pale Honey Glaze and Leaves of Thyme for a Sickabed Birthday

A light light light chiffon cake flavored and finished with the sweet outdoors.

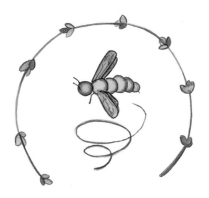

When I'm feeling puny, nothing is more reviving than scents and flavors from Mother Earth. Here is a cake that will bring pleasure to a birthday dearie sickabed on two chairs. Thyme, by the way, symbolizes courage— a pinch of which is welcome in adversity.

MAKES 10 TO 12 SERVINGS

FOR THE PAN: *a firm lump of unsalted butter*
Finely shredded zest of 2 large lemons
2 1/4 cups sifted cake flour
1 cup plus 3 tablespoons sugar
1 tablespoon baking powder
Rounded 1/4 teaspoon salt
3 fluid ounces canola, safflower, or other light flavorless oil

1/4 cup egg yolks (3 to 4 extra-large), warmed in their shells
before separating
1/2 cup cool water
1/2 cup fresh lemon juice (about 2 large lemons), at room
temperature
1 1/4 cups egg whites (8 to 9 extra-large), warmed in their shells
before separating
1/2 teaspoon fresh cream of tartar
Honey Glaze *(recipe follows)*
Rounded 1 teaspoon of fresh thyme leaves and several flowery
sprigs of thyme, for the decoration (see NOTE*)*
NOTE: *If you'd prefer, substitute flowers or petals and small*
leaves of chamomile, anise hyssop, bee balm, or fennel

TO MAKE THE CAKE, heat the oven to 325°F. Run the lump of butter over the bottom of one 10-inch tube pan, smooth in a ring of waxed paper to line the bottom, then butter the paper. Divide the lemon zest in half, reserving one part for the glaze (wrap both to keep moist). Into a large mixing bowl, sift together the flour, 1 cup of the sugar, the baking powder, and salt. Beating on low speed, in a slow steady stream add the oil, the yolks, the water, and the lemon juice. Beat just until the mixture is smooth—do not overmix. Set aside. With clean beaters, beat the whites in a large mixing bowl at low speed until frothy. Add the cream of tartar and beat on medium speed until soft peaks form. Beat on high speed while sprinkling in the remaining 3 tablespoons sugar, a tablespoon at a time. Continue beating just until the peak in the bowl holds, then flops when you lift the beaters. Add one third of the whites to the yolk mixture and blend in with a flat wire whisk or large flexible rubber spatula. Add the remaining whites and sprinkle over one portion of lemon zest. Fold the batter with a large flexible rubber spatula to finish blending thoroughly. Smooth into the pan, slightly pushing the batter up against the tube and the sides.

BAKE IN THE MIDDLE OF THE OVEN until a broomstraw or thin metal skewer emerges clean from the center, about 60 minutes. At once invert the pan and either stand it on its feet or hang from the neck of a bottle until the cake is cold. MAKE-AHEAD NOTE: Wrapped airtight and stored on the cool side of room temperature, the cake will keep fresh for 1 day.

Honey Glaze

MAKES ABOUT 1 CUP

2/3 cup delicate honey
1/4 cup granulated sugar
4 tablespoons (1/2 stick) unsalted butter
Finely shredded zest of 1 lemon (reserved when making the cake)

TO MAKE THE GLAZE, stir the honey, sugar, butter, and zest in a saucepan over low heat until the sugar has dissolved and the butter has melted. Cool slightly until thick enough to glide down the cake. MAKE-AHEAD NOTE: the glaze may be prepared up to a week in advance, refrigerated, then reheated.

TO ASSEMBLE THE CAKE, up to 6 hours before serving, set the cake on a rack over a baking sheet. Spoon the glaze over the cake, letting it drizzle down inside the center and on the outsides. Sprinkle over the thyme leaves, and when the glaze has cooled, lift the cake onto a platter. Keep on the cool side of room temperature until serving. Just before serving, wreathe sprigs around the bottom of the platter, plant a banner of greeting, and arrange the (soft green) candles. Slice with a serrated knife, and include an herbal sprig on each plate.

FOR AN ICE, refreshing golden honey, page 116.

From quiet homes and first beginning,
Out to the undiscovered ends,
There's nothing worth the wear of winning,
But laughter and the love of friends.
—HILAIRE BELLOC
Dedicatory Ode

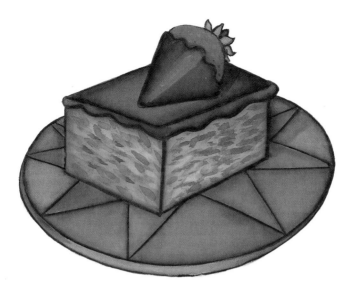

Fresh Ginger Gingercake Frosted with Glossy Chocolate and Studded with Chocolate-Dipped Fruit For A Crowd

One sumptuous layer of the old-fashioned favorite, intensely flavored and frosted and luxuriously finished.

Seek no further for Great Cake. Oh, there are cakes that are richer. Nobler. Gooier. More historied. But none is warmer, subtler, more versatile. Voluptuous. Make it simple with just whipped cream. Or make it fancy with chocolate frosting and chocolate-dipped fruit (my imaginative friend Laurie Colwin taught me the unimagined pleasure of gingercake with chocolate). But make it, especially for a crowd.

MAKES 24 TO 28 SERVINGS

FOR THE PAN: *a firm lump of unsalted butter*
4 cups all-purpose flour, lightly spooned into the cup
1/2 tablespoon plus 1/8 teaspoon baking soda
1/2 tablespoon plus 1/8 teaspoon baking powder
1/2 tablespoon finely ground white pepper
1/2 teaspoon cinnamon
1/2 teaspoon nutmeg
1/4 teaspoon ground cloves or allspice
3/4 teaspoon salt
20 tablespoons (2 1/2 sticks) unsalted butter, melted
1 1/4 cups (firmly packed) light brown sugar, lumps crushed
1/3 cup light molasses
1/3 cup dark corn syrup
1 2/3 cups boiling water
3 extra-large eggs, warmed in their shells
1 cup lightly packed minced peeled fresh ginger root, best chopped
  in a food processor or blender (buy 4 ounces or see NOTE)
Creamy Glossy Semisweet Chocolate Frosting *(recipe follows)*
Chocolate-Dipped Fruit *for the decoration (recipe follows,*
  optional)
NOTE: *If fresh ginger is unavailable, use 1/4 cup ground ginger*
and sift with the other dry ingredients.

TO MAKE THE CAKE, heat the oven to 350°F. Run the lump of butter over
the bottom of one 9-by-13-by-2-inch baking pan, smooth in a rectangle of
waxed paper, then butter the paper. Sift the flour, baking soda, baking
powder, white pepper, cinnamon, nutmeg, ground cloves, and salt together.
In a very large mixing bowl, beat the butter, sugar, molasses, corn syrup,
and boiling water on medium speed until blended. Break in the eggs and
beat until smooth. Blend in the flour in three parts (sprinkling it over the
bowl), and beat on the lowest speed manageable just until each addition
disappears, scraping the bowl occasionally. Sprinkle the fresh ginger over
the batter. Fold the batter with a large flexible rubber spatula to finish
blending thoroughly. Smooth into the pan, slightly pushing the batter up
against the sides.

BAKE IN THE MIDDLE OF THE OVEN until a toothpick emerges clean from the center, 45 to 50 minutes. Cool in the pan on a rack 15 minutes, then carefully turn the cake out, top side up, onto the rack to cool completely. MAKE-AHEAD NOTE: For the lightest cake, serve the day of baking. The cake keeps well for a week, wrapped airtight in a cool place, but each day it gets heavier, until it has completely changed character.

Creamy Glossy Semisweet Chocolate Frosting

MAKES 2 1/2 CUPS

1 1/2 cups sour cream (do not use a "light" substitute, it won't
   have enough body)
15 to 16 ounces semisweet chocolate, melted
A few grains of salt
1 1/4 teaspoons pure vanilla extract

TO MAKE THE FROSTING, use a wooden spoon to blend the sour cream with the chocolate while the chocolate is still warm, then blend in the salt and vanilla. Spread at once. MAKE-AHEAD NOTE: The frosting may be tightly covered and refrigerated a day or two, then softened over hot water until spreadable.

ChocoLate - Dipped Fruit

COVERS AT LEAST 30 PIECES
(THIS MUCH WOULD COVER MORE, BUT A GENEROUS DEPTH MAKES EASY DIPPING)

24 to 28 perfect large-bite-size pieces of an assortment of colorful fruit: unhulled strawberries, pitted unstemmed cherries, orange segments (without membrane), pineapple triangles, kiwi rounds, bias-cut banana slices, glacé apricots or pineapple or...; dry and at room temperature
12 ounces milk chocolate, finely chopped

Be aware that chocolate won't dip well in damp weather, nor in a room much above 70°F. TO DIP THE FRUIT in chocolate, have the fruit close at hand on toweling. Line a baking sheet with waxed paper. Melt the chocolate in a bowl over (not in) a pot of hot (not simmering) water, stirring constantly. (Should water splash into the chocolate, scoop out all around it and discard—water stiffens chocolate.) When melted, remove the chocolate bowl and pot from the heat, but keep them together. Stir vigorously until a drop of chocolate feels vaguely cool on the wrist (83°F). Holding the piece of fruit from the top, dip just halfway into the chocolate. Set on the baking sheet. If the chocolate should thicken while dipping, reheat the water slightly. When all the pieces are done, set the sheet in the refrigerator for just 5 minutes, then finish hardening at room temperature (60°-70°F). MAKE-AHEAD NOTE: Depending how moist the fruit and the weather, the pieces should hold nicely at least 4 and up to 12 hours.

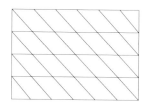

TO ASSEMBLE THE CAKE, up to 6 hours before serving, set the cake on a serving tray and smooth the frosting over the cake. With a ruler as guide, draw light lines in the frosting on top of the cake with a thin skewer. For twenty 2-by-4 1/4-inch pieces (and 8 half-diamonds for those who want "just a small piece"), draw 3 lines down the cake the long way, making 4 equal sections. Make 5 marks every 2 inches along each long side. Connect the first mark on the long side with the first line on the short side, the second mark with the second line...the fourth mark with the corner, the fifth mark with the first mark on the opposite side...and so on. (The handsomest pieces are diamonds, I think, but should you prefer 24 pieces of equal size, simply mark the cake in 2-inch squares.) Keep the cake on the cool side of room temperature. Up to 2 hours before serving, center a piece of chocolate-dipped fruit in each diamond or square, centering smaller pieces in the half-diamonds. Arrange the candles in clusters at random and plant a banner of greeting. MAKE-AHEAD NOTE: This frosting doesn't ever thoroughly set, so the cake may be frosted as soon as it has cooled, then the lines drawn hours later.

FOR AN ICE, the boldness of rum, page 116.

The custom of sending friends home from a party
with favors
is as ancient as the pharaohs,
who are said to have presented glittering gold and gems
to their honored guests.
Indeed, one of the first recorded birthday celebrations—
described in Genesis—
was given by a pharaoh.

European Water Ices

*Exceedingly light fresh tinkly crystalline crushes of
fruits, spirits, and herbs.*

These are the *granités* you'll find in cafés along the French Riviera,
becoming *granita* across the border, all through Italy.
Next to sorbets (a.k.a. sherbets), their flavors are thinner and purer.
The texture is fluffy crunchy rather than velvety smooth.
In fact, these ices are *so* slip-down-the-gullet, *so* refreshing,
that once started, it's hard to stop eating them.
If not too rich for the cake, a plop of whipped cream on the ice is luxe. At once
sophisticated and blithely simple.

ALL RECIPES MAKE FROM 5 1/2 TO 6 CUPS
(LIGHTLY PACKED), 8 TO 10 SERVINGS

Sugar Syrup for Water Ices

MAKES 4 CUPS

Scant 1 2/3 cups granulated sugar
Scant 3 1/4 cups cool water

TO MAKE THE SYRUP, combine the sugar and water and stir until clear.
MAKE-AHEAD NOTE: Refrigerated, the syrup keeps indefinitely.

Basic Recipes for Fruit Water Ices

For fruits suggested in this book.
Choose them ripe, fragrant, and richly flavored.

MAKES ABOUT 2 CUPS SMOOTH FRUIT PURÉE

Blackberries: about 3 cups
Cherries: 2 pounds, pitted
Cranberries: 1 1/2 pounds fresh or frozen
Grapes: 1 3/4 pounds Concord, Red Flame, or other richly
*   flavored colorful sort*
Peaches: 1 1/4 pounds, sliced; out of season, use best-quality
*   canned freestones*
Raspberries: about 3 cups
Strawberries: about 3 cups, hulled

2 cups smooth fruit purée
2 cups sugar syrup, page 114
3 to 7 tablespoons strained fresh lemon juice
3 tablespoons strained fresh orange juice, as needed

To PREPARE FRUIT MIXTURES FOR FREEZING, purée all fruits. Purée black-berries, raspberries, and strawberries uncooked. Purée the following after cooking with just enough water to keep from scorching: peaches, cooked just until heated through; cherries, cranberries, and grapes until tender. Purée through a food mill, or in a food processor, straining out lumps through a sieve. Blend with the sugar syrup. To emphasize flavor, for every orange, red, or blue fruit, taste as you blend in a little lemon and orange juice. For fruit that is blond, taste as you blend in lemon juice. Then does it need more sugar, lemon, a pinch or two of spice, or a splash of spirits for even greater interest? Freeze as directed on page 114. MAKE-AHEAD NOTE: The mixture may be chilled the day before freezing.

To FREEZE WATER ICES, turn the mixture into a metal pan or pans (a nonstick-coated pan is easiest), and set in the freezer. After a long hour, scrape the sides of the pan into the center with a spoon. In another hour, stir again, now chopping up blocks into bits with the edge of the spoon to make a fluffy texture and to mix the ice together. Repeat in another hour. The ice is ready to serve when completely frozen, 2 to 3 1/2 hours. Cover until serving. Should time get away from you and the ice freeze solid, whiz it in a food processor or blender or with a mixer. Rather than silvery crystals, you'll have powdered snow—a pity, but not a total loss. MAKE-AHEAD NOTE: Once the ice is fluffy, it will hold for days, with only a minimum of chopping needed at serving time. But for freshness, most water ices are best the day of freezing.

Recipe for some Water Ices from Juices, Coffee, Honey and Spirits

Combine all ingredients and freeze as directed on page 114.

APPLE OR PEAR WATER ICE

2 2/3 cups unsweetened unfiltered pure apple or pear juice (from the health food store), 1 1/3 cups sugar syrup, page 114, 1 3/4 tablespoons strained fresh lemon juice, 1 3/4 tablespoons strained fresh orange juice

GOLDEN HONEY WATER ICE

3 1/4 cups water, 1 cup light honey, 2/3 cup granulated sugar, 1/3 cup strained fresh lemon juice, and 1/4 cup strained fresh orange juice. (Honeyed mixtures can take almost twice as long to freeze as those made with sugar.)

MEYER LEMON WATER ICE

1 1/4 cups strained fresh Meyer lemon juice (or 1/2 cup plus 2 tablespoons each strained fresh basic lemon and orange juices), 1 1/2 cups sugar syrup, page 114 and 1 1/4 cups water

ORANGE WATER ICE

2 2/3 cups strained fresh orange juice, 1 1/3 cups sugar syrup, page 114, and 3 1/2 tablespoons strained fresh lemon juice (or to taste)

RUM WATER ICE

3/4 cup less 1 tablespoon dark dry rum, 3 1/4 cups sugar syrup, page 114, 1 1/2 tablespoons strained fresh lemon juice, and 1 tablespoon strained fresh orange juice

CONTINENTAL-ROAST COFFEE WATER ICE

3 cups brewed double strength roast coffee, 1 cup sugar syrup, page 114, scant 2 tablespoons strained fresh orange juice, a pinch of cinnamon

A Water Ice from Leaves

FRESH PEPPERMINT WATER ICE

3 1/4 cups boiling water, 2 to 2 1/2 tablespoons finely snipped fresh peppermint or other mint leaves, 3/4 cup plus 1 tablespoon sugar syrup, page 114, 2 tablespoons strained fresh lemon juice

TO MAKE AN INFUSION OF LEAVES FOR A WATER ICE, pour the boiling water over the leaves in a bowl, cover, and leave until cold. Strain, pressing out all the infusion in the sieve, then blend in the remaining ingredients and freeze.

> *Monday's child is fair of face,*
> *Tuesday's child is full of grace,*
> *Wednesday's child is full of woe,*
> *Thursday's child has far to go,*
> *Friday's child is loving and giving,*
> *Saturday's child works hard for a living,*
> *But the child that is born on the Sabbath*
> *Is bonny and blithe, and good and gay.*
> —OLD NURSERY RHYME

Baking Perfect Birthday Cakes At High Altitudes

I live at 5800 feet. When I can, I bake in a tube pan so the batter has a post to cling to. When I must bake in a layer pan, rich batters often sink slightly after cooling. I pay no attention, as the frosting covers the dip. Since a light moist sponge cake always falls, I make the *génoise* on page 89. It falls only a tad, and is wonderfully fine. Here are general guidelines for adapting the recipes in this book to high altitudes.

◆ FROM 3000 FEET UP: always increase oven temperature 25 degrees.

◆ FROM 3000 TO 6500 FEET: reduce baking powder from 1/8 to 1/4 teaspoon per cup of flour, reduce sugar 1 to 2 tablespoons per cup, and only if the cake proves dry, next time add 2 to 3 tablespoons liquid overall.

◆ FROM 7000 TO 10,000 FEET: reduce overall baking powder by 1/4, add 1 egg white or 1 whole egg overall, decrease sugar 2 to 3 tablespoons per cup, add 1 to 2 tablespoons flour per cup, and, in rich batters, use a few less tablespoons butter or oil overall. Apply the minimum of these changes to lower altitudes, increasing to the maximum of these changes at higher altitudes.

◆ WHEN USING BAKING SODA to neutralize buttermilk, sour milk, sour cream, cocoa, molasses, or honey: do not use less than 1/2 teaspoon soda per 1 cup of the acid ingredient.

◆ AT HIGHEST ALTITUDES, to keep great volume from coarsening the crumb, use cold eggs and underbeat them. And the *instant* your cake is cool, wrap it airtight in plastic film, then foil, then put it in a tightly sealed tin, if possible. The drying air makes mischief with a moist crumb.

> *Ah, my beloved, fill the cup that clears*
> *To-day of past Regrets and future Fears:*
> *To-morrow?—Why, To-morrow I may be*
> *Myself with Yesterday's Sev'n Thousand Years.*
> —EDWARD FITZGERALD
> *Rubáiyát of Omar Khayyám*